The Tailors *of* Tomaszow

1: My Tomaszow

Opening the wrapper of an ice-cream bar—*loda* in Polish—takes me back to my lost childhood. The ice-cream vendor with his white pushcart by the kiosk on the corner of Antoniego and Moscickiego Streets bent down and reached deep into the icy depths of his frigid treasure chest to retrieve a *Pingwin* (Penguin) bar, my favorite brand. Carefully, I would tear the paper wrapper and stare at eight ounces of chocolate-covered bliss, then slowly sink my teeth through the crunchy coating into the creamy vanilla. The world seemed perfect as I savored every bite.

Through my sixth birthday life was sweet in Tomaszow-Mazowiecki, my hometown in central Poland. Down the street from the ice-cream man's corner was beautiful Rode Park, named after a civic-minded physician who had founded our local hospital.[1] Cousin Rutka often would take me to play in the sandbox where I used shovels and pails to build castles surrounded by interconnected moats, which I'd fill with water from the park's fountains. Sometimes Cousin Fryda Tenenbaum, only ten months younger than I was, would come with her aunt Zlacia Warzecha to my house. *Tatus* ("Papa" in Polish) would order napoleons from the neighborhood pastry shop, and after a snack we went to play in the park.

Nearby was a lovely beach along the River Pilica where Tatus tried to teach me to swim by holding my body as I kicked in the water. He did all he could to please me and my brother Romek, who was two years my junior. When returning from town, Tatus frequently brought goodies for us, such as frankfurters and imported canned sprats, special treats that were my favorite foods for many years.

I loved the delightful toys Tatus bought me: a gaily painted, metal wind-up carousel whose riders flew out horizontally as they circled round and round; cardboard dolls that came with dresses, shoes, coats, hats, and pocketbooks; and a wooden ship, painted glossy blue on the sides with white portholes. On the deck sailors stood at attention dressed in blue pants and white shirts adorned with blue-trimmed collars and red bows in front. Strings stretched from the top of the ship's masts and flags down to the deck.

Tatus—Avram Chaim (Albert) Margulies—was orphaned at a very young age. In fact, he never even knew his father, Reuben Margulies, a scholar who studied the Torah (bible). Not long after marrying Rivka Jung in a customary arranged match, Reuben Margulies contracted tuberculosis. Since antibiotics were unknown at the time he succumbed and died before my father's birth on March 8, 1909, in Mogielnice, Poland. Rivka had only a few short years with her son because when Avram Chaim was just two years old she also died from the same illness.

So Papa's maternal grandparents, Shlomo and Simcha Bina Jung, raised him. They had a wholesale grain business, and as a boy Papa helped out, carrying heavy sacks of grain. Once in a while his grandfather took him to the Gerrer Rabbi, the leader of a major Hasidic sect based in the town of Góra Kalwaria, called "Ger" in Yiddish. Young Avram Chaim was well liked by all the *Chasidim* and the rabbi, Avraham Mordechai Alter, blessed him, saying, "Vilno vest du zein a gaon," meaning, "If you have the will, you will be a great man."

Greatness in the Jewish communities of Poland was typically measured by scholarly achievement in mastering Torah and Talmud (rabbinical commentary and analysis of the bible and Jewish law). But Papa chose a more practical path. Having grown up as an orphan amid challenging economic circumstances, his plan was to earn a good living as a master tailor.

So following his elementary school education, he began working as an apprentice, sewing coats and suits for a local tailor.

"He was real fast and a real good tailor, talked fast too," said Leibish Szampaner, who worked alongside Avram Chaim.

He then joined Jozef (Joseph) Tenenbaum (my mother's younger brother, who would introduce Mama to Papa), making ready-to-wear suits for shipment to Russia in Brzeziny, a small town near Lodz, which was home to many immigrants who had arrived in Poland in the 1920s.

Uncle Jozef remembered landing his job with the Brzeziny tailor Moishe Kleinbaum after his own apprenticeship in Tomaszow.

> I was reading a paper, a Jewish paper, in the classified ads. In a city nearby [Brzeziny] they are looking for tailors. So I picked up [the] newspaper and I went to that city, and I came into that place—it was a big shop, a custom-made shop. I said, "I am coming in with the ad for the job." And the boss asks me, "Are you a full-fledged tailor?" because I looked young. He didn't believe me. I said, "Try me out."
>
> Moishe Kleinbaum was the name of the tailor. There were more than ten tailors working there. He tried me out. Naturally I was good, and I was working there. He said he'll pay me thirty-five *zlotys* a week.
>
> I needed to have where to sleep. So I said to the owner, "It's not enough money." He said, "You're a nice little guy, from a nice house. Would you mind eating with me?" So I said OK. A few weeks [later] I said, "No, I can't do it any more." So I got more money. Sixty zlotys a week. It's a lot of money.
>
> I stayed there and I worked there for three years.

In 1929 the depression began taking its toll on the ready-to-wear business in Brzeziny. As orders for new clothing slowed to a trickle, Uncle Jozef and Avram Chaim were laid off. So they decided to leave Poland for France to study the latest tailoring skills and techniques in Paris.

"We planned it, we'll come back with new ideas, new styles, and come back to Tomaszow and we'll make a success," recalled Uncle Jozef.

That's exactly what happened. After graduating from Parisian tailoring school Papa and Uncle Jozef were master tailors. They opened a business together in February 1930 at number 13 Ulica Jerozolimska (Jerusalem Street), the apartment of Uncle Jozef's parents (my grandparents), Hershel Tenenbaum and Raizel Kozlowska Tenenbaum. There was much demand for their skill and talent, which made their shop, Tres Chic, an instant hit in town.

Father was always interested in the latest innovations; he wanted to be at the forefront of progress. The hottest style in men's clothing

The young tailors: (left to right) Uncle Jozef Tenenbaum and Avram Chaim "Albert" Margulies (Papa). Courtesy of Fryda Tenenbaum.

at the time showed suit jackets with padded shoulders, tapered at the waist, cut short, fitting snugly around the hips, with six buttons introducing a V opening leading to sharply pointed lapels. The jacket had a breast pocket and could be either single- or double-breasted, which was especially fashionable. Pants were cut for a high waist and loose fit—finely dressed men typically wore suspenders—with double pleats and cuffs.[2]

"New styles, new things. Naturally young people want to look good. The styles were fancy styles. Oh, they were beautiful," recalled Uncle Jozef.

The partners worked together for a year and a half until Tatus moved out on August 10, 1931, to open his own shop in a single-story building at number 21 Swietego Antoniego, apartment 1. There, Papa had the town's only neon sign, which flashed on and off, proclaiming,

> A. Margulies
> Art du Tailleur

Jozef Tenenbaum in Paris.
Courtesy of Fryda Tenenbaum.

Paryski Zakład Krawiecki
Tres Chic

(A. Margulies, The Art of Tailoring, Parisian Tailor Workshop, *Tres Chic*)

Uncle Jozef opened his own shop, named Pariski Krawiec (Parisian Tailor), where eventually he would employ a half-dozen tailors. He and Papa were just two of Tomazsow's many tailors, numbering about 300.

"There was so much competition. Everyone wanted to make a better suit than the other. It was competition all over," said Uncle Jozef.

Indeed, Father's success drew resentment. Some other tailors were so jealous that our neon sign was intentionally broken several times, though we were never certain exactly who was responsible.

Mama, Hinda (Helen or "Hela" in Polish) Tenenbaum, finished elementary school and was accepted to the Polish *gymnasium* (sec-

Hinda Tenenbaum Margulies (Mama). Courtesy of Rena Margulies Chernoff.

ondary school). Her parents, Hershel and Raizel Tenenbaum, were orthodox, observant Jews. When they found out that the gymnasium required attendance on the Sabbath, they forbade Mother from studying there. So instead of pursuing an education at the gymnasium, she opted to become a dressmaker. Consequently, both my parents began their careers in the garment industry.

Mama had the looks of a beautiful movie star. She was about five feet four inches in height, medium build, with brown, wavy hair, blue eyes, brilliant teeth, narrow lips, and a perfectly formed straight nose. What's more, she was intelligent and wise.

In Poland in the 1930s, it was customary to provide a dowry for a new bride so that she would have the wherewithal to start a home and, in many instances, also support a husband while he studied the holy books, the Torah and Talmud.

Grandpa Hershel, seeing his daughter's beauty, declared, "For you I do not have to worry about a dowry. I'm sure a suitable groom will be more than happy to get your hand in marriage without a dowry."

Grandpa was right. When Uncle Jozef brought Avram Chaim home, he set his eyes on Mama and fell in love with her. Sure

Wedding photo of Hinda Tenenbaum Margulies and Avram Chaim Margulies. Courtesy of Rena Margulies Chernoff.

enough, he was delighted to obtain her hand in marriage, not caring that Grandpa offered no financial incentive. Mama and Papa married in July of 1932 and enjoyed a very happy partnership.

A year after Mama and Papa married, I came upon the scene on July 6, 1933. I was named after my father's mother, Rivka. In Polish my name was Rena, or as everyone called me, Renia, the diminutive of Rena. In honor of my birth and to celebrate our family's joy, Father, jovial and generous, made a feast lasting several days.

As a first-born child I was showered with attention. Mother took care of me while sewing for her customers and also hired a Polish nanny to watch over me as well as clean for us, a luxury that only a few Jewish families in our community could afford. Though there was tension between Jews and Poles in Tomaszow and anti-Semitism (which I would experience only later in my sheltered childhood), my nanny, Marysia, a Catholic woman, was kind. She was about twenty years old, thin, and small in stature, with dark hair and black eyes.

Marysia lived on the top floor of a three-story house on Piliczna Street in the Karpaty neighborhood of town, a poor section that

Baby Renia with parents and grandparents. (Left to right standing) Cousin Basja Freindlich, Aunt Eva Tenenbaum, Hinda Tenenbaum-Margulies (Mama), Renia Margulies (me), Avram Chaim Margulies (Papa). (Seated) Raizel Machel Kozlowska-Tenenbaum (Grandma), Hershel Tenenbaum (Grandpa). Courtesy of Rena Margulies Chernoff.

some Jews avoided for fear of being beaten up. Once Marysia took me to her apartment to show me her Christmas tree, of which she was very proud. The tree, which she had carefully decorated, stood in the center of her living room, framed by the building's slanted ceilings.

My brother Romek, named after Papa's father Reuben, was born on August 24, 1935. A midwife came to our house for the delivery and placed a white screen around Mama's bed to provide privacy, though several close relatives surrounded her. Of course, I was accustomed to being the center of attention, especially since my crib was in Mama and Papa's bedroom. With the screen and the crowd around Mama, I felt isolated and started yelling, "Boi sie" ("I am afraid"). For a long time afterwards I had a recurring dream of my bed being at one end of a large room and a hospital bed with a white sheet around it at the other end of the room.

Romek had invaded my world. Why was he, a mere baby, the object of so much interest? His arrival was a shock, but after a few months I adjusted to the reality of having a sibling. He inherited my old crib, and Mama and Papa bought me a new wrought-iron bed with shining brass globules adorning the white frame.

Indeed, Romek became a very good brother. He was smart and sharp, just like my father, and as he grew he became my protector, coming to my rescue when other children threatened me.

Mama was an accomplished seamstress and dressmaker who employed three workers to serve her own clientele. But now with the responsibility of raising two children and my father's tailoring enterprise growing, she gave up dressmaking to concentrate on my brother and me and helping Father with his business.

In the 1930s there were no ready-made garments sold in Tomaszow's stores; all suits and coats were sewn to order. Customers came to Papa's tailor shop, which was in our apartment, described what kind of suit or coat they desired, then chose fabrics and sometimes furs as well from the selection that Papa kept on hand.

Our front door led directly to the fitting room, dominated by a large, imposing floor-to-ceiling mirror, which was framed in shining ebony, deeply carved with roses, peonies, and other flowers. At the frame's bottom, on both sides of the mirror, were small drawers for Father to store chalk, measuring tapes, and cushions stuck with dozens and dozens of pins. The windowpanes in the fitting room were made of fluted glass, allowing our customers complete privacy when they changed their clothing. White woven curtains covered the window, and a large iridescent Venetian glass beetle, blue-green with long black legs, hung on the upper panel of the curtains as a focus of interest.

Sometimes I would stand on a chair and recite poems or sing for our customers. One client brought me a beaten red-leather drawstring purse that she had purchased during a vacation in Zakopane, a resort in the Tatry mountain range of southern Poland.

While customers stood before the mirror, Tatus conducted fittings. A tape measure hung around his neck, he studied the garments with an expert's trained eye, while consulting the client on his preference as to the length of the pants and sleeves, then adjusted the garment to make sure it fit just right. No matter how peculiar a person's body and posture might be, Tatus knew how to adjust the clothing to minimize physical imperfections.

Avram Chaim "Albert" Margulies, July 23, 1938. Courtesy of Rena Margulies Chernoff.

With a pencil stuck behind his ear, he used his tape to measure the chest, waist, and hips, the shoulders, jacket length, and sleeves, first to the elbows, then to the wrist. Then he moved down to the pants, measuring the length on the outside of the leg to the top of the shoe, and then on the inside, from the crotch to the shoe top. Mother generally stood by and wrote the measurements in a notebook as Father announced them. When Mama was not around, Tatus recorded the information in the notebook himself.

After measuring, Papa cut the fabric to his customer's dimensions. Tailors in the workshop stitched canvas on the lapels, collar, and front of the garment to give the fabric body; then they basted the front portion of the garment to the back and to the sleeves. After basting, the customer came in for a first fitting. Father made all the necessary alterations to be sure the garment would fit well, then scheduled an appointment for a second fitting.

In the course of the second fitting, he made final adjustments to the garment, double-checking the length of the sleeves and pants.

The customer, viewing himself in our full-length mirror, saw how the garment fit and envisioned how it would look upon completion. Father informed the customer when the clothing would be finished and ready to be picked up.

In addition to assisting with fittings, Mama kept the books and accounts for the business. When Papa had a hernia operation she ran the shop singlehandedly, taking measurements for suits and coats, cutting the fabric and fitting garments on customers until Papa recovered and was well enough to resume work.

Beyond the foyer was our bedroom, a cheerful room with the sun shining in the morning through white tailored curtains onto our beige furniture. In the winter my parents used a down quilt to cover themselves. When making the double bed in the morning, Mother put a wooden form on top of the quilt to make the bed appear perfectly even and tailored and on top placed a shining satin yellow bedspread. The form was made of wooden boards about two inches in width and one-half inch in height that crisscrossed to create square patterns. Hinges connected the squares in several places so the form could be folded and stored when not in use at night. Two night tables flanked the bed, and an armoire and chest completed the set. My crib was located at the far end of the bedroom.

To the left of the foyer was our kitchen. Cabinets, cupboards, and credenzas for dishes, utensils, as well as pots and pans, lined the walls, surrounding a dining table and chairs. On one wall of the kitchen was a rectangular black-iron coal stove, which had a range with four heating units, an oven for baking, and a built-in container for heating water. Mama and Papa heated the stove with kindling and added coke or coal to keep the fire going from morning through evening.

Once a month a truck filled with coal made a delivery to our house. Workers attached a chute from the truck to a window in the cellar and coal poured out down the chute. Once, when one of Father's tailors, Israel "Srulek" Rozanski, went down to the cellar to fetch some coal, I followed and saw to my amazement a large black mountain lying in one corner of the cellar. We used coal not only for cooking but also for heating the home and the irons. Later on Tatus would switch to electric-powered irons.

As our workers arrived in the morning, Father asked whether

they had eaten breakfast. Those who had not would join us at the kitchen table.

Past the kitchen was our workshop, packed with Singer sewing machines, a large table for cutting fabrics, heavy irons and ironing boards, and a headless dummy. Boards with damp furs nailed to them were left to stretch and dry, and bales of fabric lay on the shelves, part of Papa's large selection of material from which customers could choose for their suits and coats. In a separate room were additional sewing supplies, threads, linings, canvas, and in the cellar Tatus kept more material, trimming, padding, and buttons.

Among Papa's clients were some of the most prominent residents of Tomaszow, factory owners, lawyers, doctors, and even nobility. Once during the winter Papa took Romek and me along to Count Jan Ostrowski's home when he went to deliver several suits and coats and fit new garments for the count. We rode through Count Ostrowski's estate in a large, shining, black-and-red sled, pulled by a pair of horses that Tatus had hired. Our sleigh bells tinkled with a fine, delicate sound that broke the calm silence of the pristine woods. Icicles hanging from thin pine needles shone and sparkled as fine flakes fell silently on the snow-covered road of the count's estate. That beautiful scene—so long ago—captures the wonderful life I had with my family during my early childhood and the promise it held. But the extreme cruelty and hatred of the Nazis and Hitler would unalterably change our lives from idyllic to tragic.

Before she married, Mama taught dressmaking to her sister Eva Tenenbaum. But now Tatus advised Aunt Eva to work for him. He taught her how to make vests, promising it would be more lucrative than dressmaking.

"I made nice money, just like the men in the shop, because at that time I was very fast. I used to make two vests, custom vests, in one day," said Eva.

Papa employed a dozen workers, each specializing in a specific aspect of suit manufacturing. His apprentice was Srulek Rozanski, with whom he signed a contract promising to teach him the art of tailoring within a period of three years as required by the tailors' guild.

Though our family spoke Polish in the house, a reflection of the fact that we were among the more modern wave of Polish Jews, the

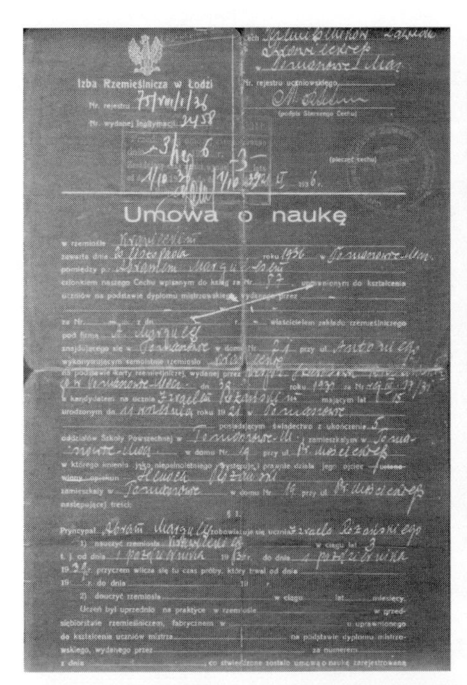

Izba Rzemieślnicza w Łodzi

Nr. rejestru 75/VIII/1/36

Nr. wydanej legitymacji 2458

Nr. rejestru uczniowskiego

(podpis Starszego Cechu)

(pieczęć cechu)

Umowa o naukę

w rzemiośle
zawarta dnia 26 listopada roku 1936 w Tomaszowie-Maz.
pomiędzy p. Abramem Margulies
członkiem naszego Cechu wpisanym do ksiąg za Nr. 57 uprawnionym do kształcenia uczniów na podstawie dyplomu mistrzowskiego, wydanego przez
za Nr. z dn. r. — właścicielem zakładu rzemieślniczego
pod firmą A. Margulies
znajdującego się w Tomaszowie w domu Nr. 24 przy ul. Antoniego
wykonywującym samoistnie rzemiosło
na podstawie karty rzemieślniczej, wydanej przez
dn. roku 1930 za Nr.
a kandydatem na ucznia Izraelem Rozańskim majacym lat 15
urodzonym dn. 11 kwietnia roku 1921 w Tomaszowie
posiadającym świadectwo z ukończenia 5
oddziałów Szkoły Powszechnej w Tomaszowie-M. zamieszkałym w Tomaszowie-Maz. w domu Nr. 14 przy ul.
w którego imieniu jako niepełnoletniego występuje, prawnie działa jego ojciec Henoch Rozański
zamieszkały w Tomaszowie w domu Nr. 14 przy ul.
następującej treści:

§ 1.

Pryncypał Abram Margulies zobowiązuje się ucznia Izraela Rozańskiego
1) nauczyć rzemiosła w ciągu lat 3
t. j. od dnia 1 października 19 36 r. do dnia 1 października
19 39 r. przyczem wlicza się tu czas próby, który trwał od dnia
19 r. do dnia 19 r.
2) douczyć rzemiosła w ciągu lat miesięcy.
Uczeń był uprzednio na praktyce w rzemiośle w przedsiębiorstwie rzemieślniczem, fabrycznem w u uprawnionego do kształcenia uczniów mistrza na podstawie dyplomu mistrzowskiego, wydanego przez za numerem
z dnia co stwierdzone zostało umową o naukę zarejestrowaną

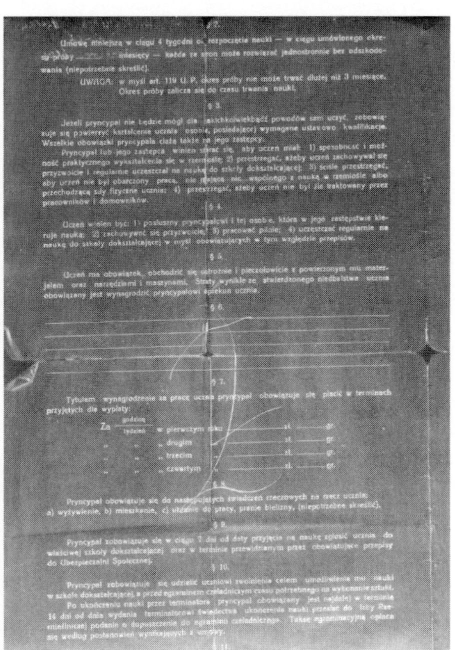

§ 2.

Umowę niniejszą w ciągu 4 tygodni od rozpoczęcia nauki — w ciągu umówionego okresu próby miesięcy — każda ze stron może rozwiązać jednostronnie bez odszkodowania (niepotrzebne skreślić).

UWAGA: w myśl art. 119 U. P. okres próby nie może trwać dłużej niż 3 miesiące. Okres próby zalicza się do czasu trwania nauki.

§ 3.

Jeżeli pryncypał nie będzie mógł dla jakichkolwiekbądź powodów sam uczyć, zobowiązuje się powierzyć kształcenie ucznia osobie, posiadającej wymagane ustawowo kwalifikacje. Wszelkie obowiązki pryncypała ciążą także na jego zastępcy.

Pryncypał lub jego zastępca winien starać się, aby uczeń miał: 1) sposobność i możność praktycznego wykształcenia się w rzemiośle; 2) przestrzegać, żeby uczeń zachowywał się przyzwoicie i regularnie uczęszczał na naukę do szkoły dokształcającej; 3) ściśle przestrzegać, aby uczeń nie był obarczony pracą, nie mającą nic wspólnego z nauką w rzemiośle albo przechodzącą siły fizyczne ucznia; 4) przestrzegać, żeby uczeń nie był źle traktowany przez pracowników i domowników.

§ 4.

Uczeń winien być: 1) posłuszny pryncypałowi i tej osobie, która w jego zastępstwie kieruje nauką; 2) zachowywać się przyzwoicie; 3) pracować pilnie; 4) uczęszczać regularnie na naukę do szkoły dokształcającej w myśl obowiązujących w tym względzie przepisów.

§ 5.

Uczeń ma obowiązek, obchodzić się ostrożnie i pieczołowicie z powierzonym mu materjałem oraz narzędziami i maszynami. Straty wynikłe ze stwierdzonego niedbalstwa ucznia obowiązany jest wynagrodzić pryncypałowi opiekun ucznia.

§ 6.

§ 7.

Tytułem wynagrodzenia za pracę ucznia pryncypał obowiązuje się płacić w terminach przyjętych dla wypłaty:

Za godzinę / tydzień w pierwszym roku zł. gr.
„ „ „ drugim zł. gr.
„ „ „ trzecim zł. gr.
„ „ „ czwartym zł. gr.

§ 8.

Pryncypał obowiązuje się do następujących świadczeń rzeczowych na rzecz ucznia: a) wyżywienie, b) mieszkanie, c) ubranie do pracy, pranie bielizny, (niepotrzebne skreślić).

§ 9.

Pryncypał zobowiązuje się w ciągu 7 dni od daty przyjęcia na naukę zgłosić ucznia do właściwej szkoły dokształcającej oraz w terminie przewidzianym przez obowiązujące przepisy do Ubezpieczalni Społecznej.

§ 10.

Pryncypał zobowiązuje się udzielić uczniowi zwolnienia celem umożliwienia mu nauki w szkole dokształcającej, a przed egzaminem czeladniczym czasu potrzebnego na wykonanie sztuki.

Po ukończeniu nauki przez terminatora pryncypał obowiązany jest najdalej w terminie 14 dni od dnia wydania terminatorowi świadectwa ukończenia nauki przesłać do Izby Rzemieślniczej podanie o dopuszczenie do egzaminu czeladniczego. Taksę egzaminacyjną opłaca się według postanowień wynikających z umowy.

§ 11.

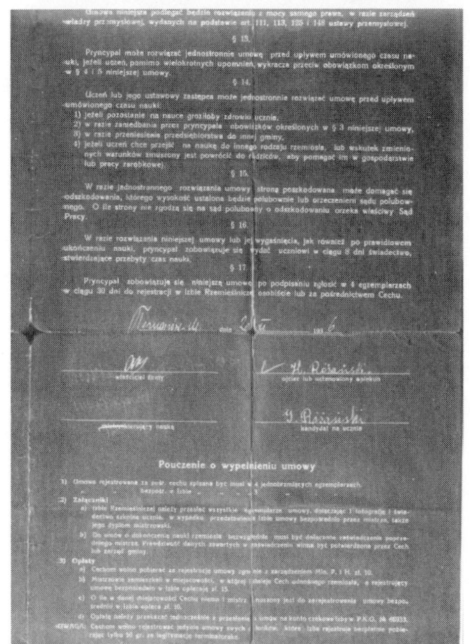

Umowa niniejsza podlegać będzie rozwiązaniu z mocy samego prawa, w razie zarządzeń władzy przemysłowej, wydanych na podstawie art. 111, 113, 125 i 148 ustawy przemysłowej.

§ 13.

Pryncypał może rozwiązać jednostronnie umowę przed upływem umówionego czasu nauki, jeżeli uczeń, pomimo wielokrotnych upomnień, wykracza przeciw obowiązkom określonym w § 4 i 5 niniejszej umowy.

§ 14.

Uczeń lub jego ustawowy zastępca może jednostronnie rozwiązać umowę przed upływem umówionego czasu nauki:
1) jeżeli pozostanie na nauce groziłoby zdrowiu ucznia,
2) w razie zaniedbania przez pryncypała obowiązków określonych w § 3 niniejszej umowy,
3) w razie przeniesienia przedsiębiorstwa do innej gminy,
4) jeżeli uczeń chce przejść na naukę do innego rodzaju rzemiosła, lub wskutek zmienionych warunków zmuszony jest powrócić do rodziców, aby pomagać im w gospodarstwie lub pracy zarobkowej.

§ 15.

W razie jednostronnego rozwiązania umowy strona poszkodowana może domagać się odszkodowania, którego wysokość ustalona będzie polubownie lub orzeczeniem sądu polubownego. O ile strony nie zgodzą się na sąd polubowny o odszkodowaniu orzeka właściwy Sąd Pracy.

§ 16.

W razie rozwiązania niniejszej umowy lub jej wygaśnięcia, jak również po prawidłowem ukończeniu nauki, pryncypał zobowiązuje się wydać uczniowi w ciągu 8 dni świadectwo, stwierdzające przebyty czas nauki.

§ 17.

Pryncypał zobowiązuje się niniejszą umowę po podpisaniu zgłosić w 4 egzemplarzach w ciągu 30 dni do rejestracji w Izbie Rzemieślniczej osobiście lub za pośrednictwem Cechu.

Tomaszów-M. dnia 26/XI 1936

właściciel firmy — ojciec lub ustanowiony opiekun H. Rozański

kierujący nauką — kandydat na ucznia I. Rozański

Pouczenie o wypełnieniu umowy

1) Umowa rejestrowana za pośr. cechu spisana być musi w 4 jednobrzmiących egzemplarzach.

2) Załączniki

3) Opłaty

(a, b, c). Employment contract between Avram Chaim Margulies and his apprentice Srulek Rozanski, dated November 26, 1936 (covering October 1, 1936–October 1, 1939). Courtesy of Rena Margulies Chernoff.

language of the shop was Yiddish. Throughout our apartment Papa's tailors sat, conversing in Yiddish, as they created the finest garments in town.

"It was a real busy shop," recalled Srulek. "Six days a week."

"[Mr. Margulies] gave out work to contractors for pants, jackets, vests. Forty-five zlotys for a suit just for the labor, plus the cost of the fabric, plus lining. It cost sixty zlotys for an overcoat. They were very expensive."

"Everything was as a 'French system.' It was good. We made about fifteen suits a week. It was a lot," said Srulek.

On top of our armoire we kept large bottles of homemade wine. Mama and Papa filled three- and five-gallon bottles with grapes, then poured sugar on top and let the mixture stand at room temperature to ferment for several months until it was ready to drink. My parents as well as my grandfather would prepare the wine after the fall grape harvest so it would be ready by spring for Passover.

One evening in 1937 Mama and Papa went out to the movies. Itzhak Hun, an employee who liked to joke and fool around, wanted to taste the wine that stared so invitingly at him from above the armoire. As Itzhak grabbed a bottle, it slipped from his hands and crashed to the floor, spilling all over. He and the other workers quickly wiped up the spilled wine. But when Mama and Papa returned home the fragrance of wine whiffed throughout the house. It did not take them long to discover from whence the smell originated. Though the employees wouldn't reveal the culprit, my parents deduced anyway that Itzhak Hun was responsible for the transgression because he was apt to play jokes and be mischievous. This incident was a subject of great amusement for our employees and was narrated often to the hilarity of all.

The atmosphere was often lighthearted in Uncle Jozef's shop as well where there was much camaraderie among the workers.

"I used to love to be in the workshop," said Fryda. "His assistants would joke and sing and do fun stuff especially when I was around."

In 1935, when I was two years old, Papa's sister Aunt Pesa died. Her fifteen-year-old, eldest daughter, Hanka Lew, came to live in our house to care for me and learn tailoring in Papa's workshop. Three years later, Hanka's younger sister, thirteen-year-old Rutka, joined our household as well. At that point Hanka was working in Papa's tailor shop so Rutka helped watch Romek and me.

In der Gas or Iber der Brik

There were two main sections of Tomaszow: *in der gas* and *iber der brik,* as they were called in Yiddish, "in the street" and "over the bridge."

Living "in the street" didn't imply "homeless," as it might seem. To the contrary, living *in der gas* meant "in town," where we resided, which was generally more prestigious than *iber der brik* (though no doubt some *iber der brik* Tomaszowers would argue otherwise).

Tomaszow-Mazowiecki is in the Mazowsze region of central Poland, seventy miles southwest of Warsaw and about thirty miles southeast of Lodz. Believe it or not, there is another Tomaszow in Poland, the far smaller Tomaszow-Lubelski of the Lublin region.

According to the 1931 census, the last one taken before World War II, Tomaszow-Mazowiecki was home to 11,310 Jews—or Tomaszowers, as we call ourselves—thirty percent of the municipality's population. But during the war, as Jews from smaller surrounding communities were forced to our town, the Jewish population

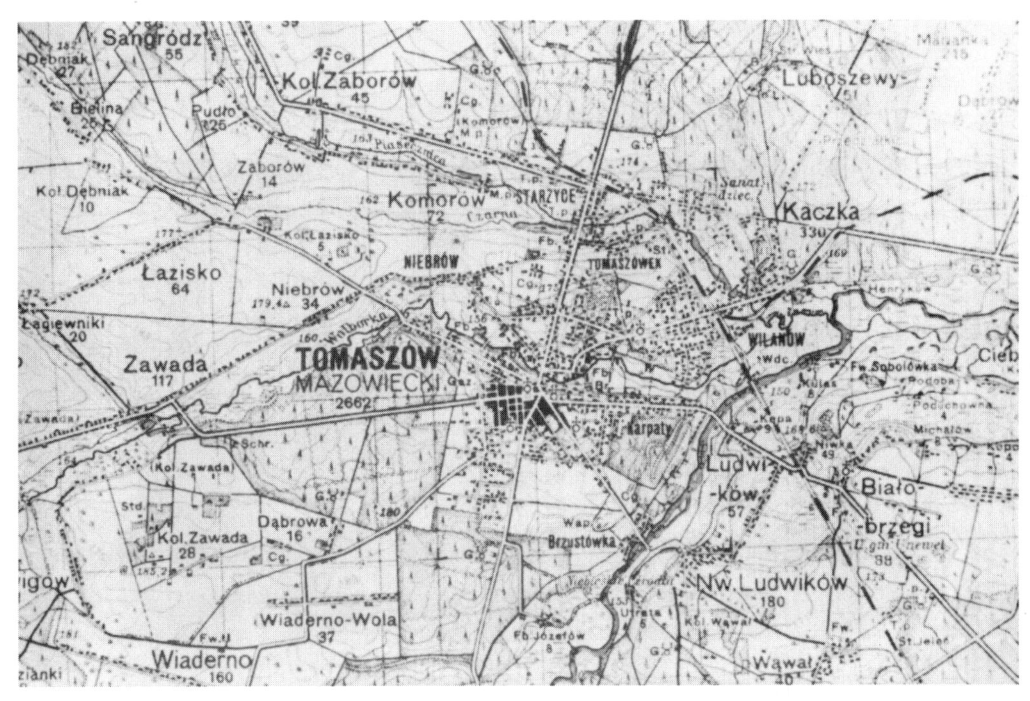

Map of Tomaszow-Mazowiecki, located in central Poland, 70 miles southwest of Warsaw

swelled to over 14,000, comprising nearly one-third of Tomaszow's 45,000 residents.

One-third of the Jews lived *iber der brik*; the remainder *in der gas.* The *brik*, or bridge, spanned the Wolborka River, one of three waterways running through Tomaszow, the others being the Pilica and the Czarna Rivers. Together they helped to fuel the textile mills that were the backbone of the town's economy.

While Tomaszow grew around the textile business, its first major factory was an iron foundry that Tomasz Adam Ostrowski built in 1789, leading to the establishment of the community. It was Ostrowski's son, Antony, who in 1822 named the town Tomaszow after his father, began developing a textile industry, and invited Jewish weavers and entrepreneurs to settle there.

In the 1880s David Bornstein established a major textile mill in Tomaszow—*iber der brik*—among the relatively few large Jewish-owned enterprises. In 1910 the French company Wilanow opened an artificial silk factory just outside of town, also *iber der brik*. It was to become the largest employer in the region; by the mid-1930s approximately 10,000 people worked in the factory, which exported fabric to countries as far away as Japan.

Though Wilanow was a major employer, it was difficult for Jews to land jobs there. The director of the factory, Mr. Hertz, had been Jewish but converted to Catholicism, and he encouraged other Jews to do the same, according to Tomaszower Nacia Shulmeister.

"In general they wouldn't take Jewish people to work there. Most of the people working in the factory were Poles. All the engineers [who landed jobs there] had to convert from Judaism to Catholicism," said Nacia. "Women had to sleep with someone to get a job, to work in Wilanow."

It was also difficult landing a job at the Bornstein factory, which produced fine wools for men's suits and winter garments. But there was none of the anti-Semitism that existed at the Wilanow factory. In fact, the owner, David Bornstein, was an Orthodox Jew, and another Jew, Herman Weinberger, was the manager. Bornstein encouraged his workers to practice their faith.

"The owners were ultra-religious people. They were ultra-religious to the point that they had established in the building where they had the offices a *shtibel* [small synagogue], and they used to *daven* [pray]," remembered Tomaszow resident Fishel Samelson.

Bornstein factory. Courtesy of Tomaszow-Mazowiecki Yizkor Book.

"They had a room or two that they gave to the people to *daven* on *Shabbos* [Sabbath]."

Tomaszow's third large industrial plant was the Landsberg factory, also located *iber der brik*, which manufactured woolen cloth for the Polish army.

Employees of the factories, particularly the well-paid engineers, were good clients of the tailors in town, having their suits made at some of the leading shops, including Papa's and Uncle Jozef's.

In general, though, many of the town's tailors were just scraping by.

"There were more tailors than customers in Tomaszow," joked Zlacia Warzecha. It was, in fact, one reason that many of those "with a trade" still struggled to earn a living. By Wednesday many Tomaszowers would worry what food they would have to put on their Sabbath table.

Indeed, Mama's childhood home had only three beds to sleep her parents and their four children.

"We were very poor. At home six people; it was very hard. Many times when I was small I was sleeping with my father in bed. Later on I slept with my brother, sisters slept with each other, and youngest slept with the mother," said Uncle Jozef.

The family quarters were tight as well at Sala Kenigsztejn's house on Warszawska Street, *iber der brik*.

"We had two big rooms for ten people . . . two to a bed; I slept with one sister, Rujah," Sala fondly recalled. "It was a poor life, but a happy life."

The Tenenbaum family, Tomaszow, June 4, 1926. Left to right standing, Hinda Tenebaum, Jozef Tenenbaum, and Rivka Tenenbaum. Seated, Raizel Machel Kozlowska-Tenenbaum, Eva Tenenbaum, and Hershel Tenenbaum. Courtesy of Rena Margulies Chernoff.

Most Tomaszowers used outhouses, as we did, and relied on *wassen tragers*, water carriers, who brought water from a well to the home carrying pails on either end of a long stick supported by their shoulders. We were fortunate enough to have a water pump in the back yard, but our apartment building had neither running water nor flush toilets, which were luxuries for the well-to-do.

Bathing at the public bathhouse, *iber der brik,* at Wesowa Street, cost fifty *grosz* (cents). A *mikveh,* a ritual bath, was located there as well.

To help alleviate poverty, Tomaszow's Jewish community established a Free Loan Society (*Gemilat Hesed*), which offered not just money but all sorts of assistance to people in need. Struggling businessmen also could receive a loan from the *Bank Kupiecki,* which opened in 1928.

My Grandparents

Grandpa Hershel Tenenbaum, Mama's father, was a handsome, tall man, standing more than six feet. They called him "der Hoiche Hersh" ("Hersh, the tall"). He wore a well-kept white beard, about five inches long, and had gentle blue eyes, a calm countenance, and a good-natured disposition. He was a weaver who worked in the artificial silk factory in town owned by Mr. Berl Blacharowicz.

Grandpa Hersh was an observant Jew who prayed twice a day, in the morning and evening. On the Sabbath afternoon he and his friends would gather on Bozniczna Street to study Talmud, the rabbinical analysis and commentary on the Bible and Jewish law, including the tractates, "Maor Vashemesh" ("From Light and Sun") and "Or Hahayim" ("The Light of Life"), major works on Chasidic ideology, which had a large following in Poland, as well as the writings of the great scholar Rashi.

Occasionally Grandpa smoked a cigarette. He stuffed loose tobacco into a thin piece of paper, rolled it, and moistened the edges with his saliva to glue the cigarette together. Later on he used a new contraption for making cigarettes. He carefully placed tobacco into thin paper lining one part of the brass tubing. A second brass tube then enveloped the first, compressing the tobacco inside the paper. Finally, using a thin metal cylinder Grandpa pushed out his home-produced cigarette.

One day my grandfather came home and announced to his oldest daughter, Rivka: "You have become a *kalah* [bride]."

"A what?" responded Rivka.

"My brother Manolo and I agreed to betroth you to his son Mordechai Hersz."

"You did what?"

Though Rivka was not happy about this agreement, there was little that she could do. A word was a word, and Grandpa Hersh would not go back on his word. Rivka married her cousin Mordechai. Shortly after the wedding they settled in Lodz, near Uncle Manolo, Mordechai's father. Soon thereafter, Uncle Manolo, Mordechai, and Rivka left Poland and emigrated to Argentina. Rivka's brother Zalman Icio soon followed. My grandparents were saddened that their daughter and son had left for Argentina, but eventually, after World War II broke out, they were glad that at least two of their children had been able to save themselves and avoid suffering through the Holocaust.

My maternal grandmother, Raizel Kozlowska Tenenbaum, known as Raizel Machel, meaning Raizel the daughter of Machel, was kind and cheerful. She was short, about five feet tall, of medium build, and had blue eyes that were framed by silver-colored wire glasses. Like her husband, she had a calm demeanor; never did I hear her talk in a loud voice. She was deeply religious and wore a dark-brown wig to cover her head in public, as was the custom for married women signifying modesty, or *tsniut*. Grandma Raizel owned a grocery store where she sold all kinds of food supplies from produce to bulk staples to baked goods.

Romek and I frequently went to Grandma's house to show her our new clothes or just to spend time with her. She listened attentively to what we said and slowly answered all kinds of questions we posed. Grandma Raizel always had a supply of homemade snacks for us, such as mandel bread and rugelach with milk. Another treat was in the garden—seckle pears that fell from a tree just to the left of the house. They were soft and succulent, rich with juice.

After her parents, Zlata Blacharowicz and Machel Kozlowski, passed away, Grandma inherited their house at number 7 Ulica Bozniczna so she and Grandpa moved there. I remember that house well. A large front yard set the wooden, ranch-style house back from the street. My grandparents lived in the front portion, and in the back, where there was a separate entrance, dwelled our cousins Chana and Josel Weisbard with their three daughters, Lola, Mania, and Edzia, who was learning to be a hatmaker. Josel Weisbard was away the whole week selling fabrics and piece goods, though not very successfully. Instead of cash he often took a credit note. Sometimes he had no money and would ask Grandpa for a loan and then forget to pay it back.

When Grandma Raizel and Grandpa Hersh moved to number 7 Bozniczna, they gave up the grocery store business. Grandma Raizel now occupied herself exclusively with selling piece goods at her stall on Plac Kosciuszki, where public market days were held on Tuesdays and Fridays. There were many merchants there hawking all kinds of products. One could buy ribbons, laces, buttons, fabrics, costume jewelry, and a broad assortment of bric-a-brac for the house. Farmers sold their chickens and produce, tomatoes, potatoes, corn, carrots, onions, herbs, as well as dairy products, butter, milk, eggs, and farmer cheese displayed on and wrapped in large green bay leaves that kept the cheese cool and made for an attractive presentation. I would walk among the stalls, fascinated with the wide

Eva Tenenbaum and Meylekh Plachta. Courtesy of Rena Margulies Chernoff.

range of merchandise, the crowds, and the intense haggling between shoppers and merchants.

Aunt Eva as a young child traveled each week with Grandma Raizel to Lodz, the large city about thirty miles northwest of Tomaszow. There Grandma paid wholesale prices for fabrics that she would then sell at her market stall. She would prepare for market days beforehand, making sure she had an adequate supply of material that was folded in an orderly manner and displayed attractively.

Once a week Grandma Raizel would load her merchandise on a wagon and travel to Ujazd, a small town six miles from Tomaszow, where she would sell her piece goods at the town's weekly market.

She was a good-hearted woman. Every Thursday she performed selfless acts of charity, collecting money from wealthy people in town and giving it to poor people she knew so they could purchase food for the Sabbath.

Eva's Wedding

Mama's younger sister Eva was my favorite aunt. Whenever she came to our house she would bring me Wedla chocolates, a well-known brand in Poland. I insisted that Eva feed me and refused food from everyone else.

Though Papa employed Eva, she worked out of her parents' apartment since our workshop was fully occupied with employees and machinery.

When I was five years old, Aunt Eva married Meylekh Plachta. Eva chose her own husband rather than submitting to an arranged marriage like her older sister Rivka and in spite of her parents' objections that Meylekh's reputation for flirting with women would place Eva in an unhappy partnership.

Meylekh was known as a "Don Juan." He was attractive, charming, and an accomplished dancer. And he was interested in Eva. One day at a dance he took Eva's purse and refused to return it unless she agreed to go out with him. Eva tried by all means to retrieve it, even begging girlfriends to intervene. Finally, after much negotiating, Meylekh returned the purse when Eva agreed to a date, which led to an intriguing courtship. After a while Eva agreed to marry Meylekh. As it turned out, he was a model husband, a most loyal and affectionate partner, who was very good to Eva.

Grandpa and Grandma overcame their objections and hosted Eva and Meylekh's wedding at their house.

For the wedding Aunt Eva wore an ankle-length, royal-blue-lace dress over salmon-colored satin lining. Mama wore a black-lace dress lined with the same salmon satin fabric. Papa dressed in black tails. Romek wore black velvet short pants and a matching velvet vest, a salmon satin shirt with ruffles around the collar and cuffs, white knee socks, and patent leather black shoes. My outfit matched Romek's, except I wore a black velvet skirt rather than pants.

It was a festive affair. The house was packed with relatives, neighbors, and friends. My grandparents hired two fiddlers, Yaakove Shaul, known as Shulik, and Avraham Bas, as well as Josef Marshalik, a *badhen*—a wedding singer—to amuse and entertain the guests.[3] Marshalik sang rhymes he wrote specifically for the couple. Tomaszow being a rather small, self-contained community, Marshalik knew the bride and groom, allowing him to intertwine his ditties with personal details. When he began to sing, the guests became absolutely silent.

"Be careful, young bride, your beloved has been known to like fun and women. Pray hard that your life should be blessed with happiness and sorrow should not cross your threshold," sang the badhen to Aunt Eva.

Josef Marshalik then addressed Meylekh the groom, warning him to seek repentance for his sins and misdeeds because his future life depended on receiving a pardon. This made the groom cry, which in turn triggered loud weeping from some relatives and other guests. Once Marshalik saw tears rolling down from the groom's eyes, he solemnly sang that the groom's tears had caused heaven above to forgive all his sins. The groom's soul had been cleansed; he had been granted a pardon and would live with his beloved in joy and happiness to a ripe old age!

Aunt Eva was very much in love with Meylekh, who was fun, loving, and kind, and they were very happy. Once he came to our house on a Saturday morning to serve us breakfast in bed, delicious warm rolls covered with butter and hot milk.

Eva and Meylekh shared an apartment at number 14 Ulica Antoniego with his widowed mother, Hene-Mirel, a short, thin, and kind lady who Eva said was very smart, which was why they got along so well.

School

In pre-war Poland the government sponsored traditional public schools whose curriculum typically included Catholic teachings, but in our neighborhood the majority of students were Jewish, one of two sections of Tomaszow where Jewish children dominated the classroom.

At the age of five I started kindergarten. Schools were identified by their principals so my school, on Pilsudskiego Street *in der gas,* was known as the Zylberowa School, since Mrs. Zylberowa ("Silver") was the principal.

Each morning as we walked to school, Mama would patiently allow me to climb and walk along brick fences in front of homes on the way. I especially enjoyed balancing myself on an incline abutting one of the buildings.

Zylberowa School, fourth grade. (Srulek Rozanski, second from left, second row; Josef Zamulewicz, third from left, second row), Tomaszow-Mazowiecki, 1934. Courtesy of Josef Zamulewicz.

My kindergarten class of about ten children had both a teacher and an assistant. We sat on small chairs at our child-size tables, where we drew pictures, colored, and sang songs. We also played in the yard and had fun with blocks, trains, and dolls. Our midmorning snack was milk and a biscuit, though I did not care much for milk.

One day the entire class was planning to view the burial of a dead bird that had been found in the schoolyard. It was a big event. The assistant teacher insisted that I finish drinking my cup of milk before she would let me go out to view the bird's burial, but once she saw that I truly could not finish the milk, she relented and allowed me to join the other children in the schoolyard. A teacher dug a grave in the soil, placed the bird in the hole, then covered it up and added a marker to indicate the bird's place of rest.

Once we staged a play about the twelve months of the year. I

Jewish gymnasium, Tomaszow-Mazowiecki. Courtesy of Tomaszow-Mazowiecki Yizkor Book.

was the month of March. Mother made me a white appliquéd dress with green grass around the hem; from the soil grew a brown tree with green leaves. I was very proud to recite several sentences about the rainy, windy month.

Even in elementary school teachers specialized: Mrs. Rubinek and Mrs. Zemanska were the homeroom teachers; Mr. Tirkiszer taught earth science and geography; Mr. Meldung was the music and religion teacher. For many of the boys that was only the beginning of their religious education. At 2 p.m. when public school ended, those boys were off to *cheder* (literally "room," a Jewish religious school), where they would learn Torah and Talmud.

Though it was predominantly a Jewish public school, Polish was the language of the classroom. This presented a problem for some children who had grown up in traditional families where Yiddish was the language spoken at home.

"When I was a young child . . . I spoke only Jewish [Yiddish]," explained Nacia Schulmeister. "I went to school, I had very bad marks." Once her Polish improved, Nacia's grades rose, allowing her to attend designing school following her elementary education.

Some Jewish children who lived *iber der brik*, including Sala

Kenigsztejn and Nuta Romer, attended a public school that had both Jewish and gentile students—the Glogowski School, where Shmuel Glogowski was principal.

Public elementary school was free in Tomaszow (though one did have to buy books), and most students attended through the sixth grade. But only a select few of Tomaszow's Jews went on to *gymnasium* (secondary school). For that you had to pay tuition, which few Tomaszowers could afford, particularly due to an arbitrary pricing schedule.

"They had a system," said Fishel (Felix) Samelson. "The committee, they set the tuition by way of thinking of what the parents can afford. In other words, they said, 'His father, being he is in business, he can afford to pay. Instead of $75 he can pay $100 or $125.' It was just the opposite. My father couldn't afford it."

Because many parents lacked the means to send their children on to gymnasium after elementary school, they advised them to "learn a trade." For the Jews of Tomaszow that often meant tailoring.

"I would have loved to go to school had it not been for the way they determined tuition," explained Fishel. "But when a boy [is] twelve, thirteen, fourteen years old and he couldn't go to school there were three things. Either he became a baker, that was a lower level, or he became a shoemaker, which was a little bit higher, or he became a tailor, which was even that much higher considered. That's how it was. Oh, there were other trades that people had. But these are the trades that people knew, associated with."

Textile mills were the largest industry in town so there was demand for craftsmen who could transform fabric into garments, and for the Jews of Tomaszow tailoring was a viable career choice at a time when options were limited, largely due to anti-Semitism. Consequently, even some with higher ambitions ended up as tailors.

"We could not be a pilot, you could not be an engineer," recalled tailor Josef Zamulewicz. "If you wanted to be a doctor you had to go overseas to study, had to study in Italy or in Vienna or Czechoslovakia. You couldn't choose whatever you want to have. So, what could you be? A tailor, a shoemaker, a carpenter. Everything was restricted for the Jewish people."

"A Jew wasn't working for the state or the city. So you were a tailor, a shoemaker. They wouldn't hire a Jew for a government job," explained Srulek Rozanski. So, at thirteen he began apprenticing with my father. At the same time he went three times a week, three hours each day, to a trade school, located at number 4 Tkacka Street.

"They called it Tkacka 4 School. It was a school for all trades: tailors, shoemakers, hatmakers, belt makers, bakers, all kinds of trades, electrician, plumber, carpenter, watchmaker. Just about everyone, ninety percent, went there, unless people studied for bookkeeping," said Srulek. "I apprenticed for three years. It wasn't steady pay. For three years you had to work for nothing. If you were lucky, the boss liked you, he gave you a bit of money.

Uncle Jozef also began as an apprentice after elementary school:

> Somehow I felt I had a talent for that. I liked nice things. I liked nice, beautiful things.
>
> I went to a tailor. Yankel Lask was the name of the tailor. He was a very good tailor, custom-made tailor.
>
> An apprentice usually had to go for three years as an apprentice. I didn't want to stay three years. So, the tailor [said I] had to pay 150 zlotys in order he should let me learn the trade faster.
>
> When you worked for three years you had to take care of the children, draw up the water, it took a lot and then after the three years you didn't know so much. So this way after I paid him, he sat you down and showed you.
>
> That was a lot of money in that time. In two years I learned the trade. I was sixteen years of age. I was a full-fledged tailor. I knew already. But I looked young also. After I finished these two years I said to the boss, he should pay. So he said, "I cannot pay you too much. I can give you fifteen zlotys a week." It wasn't too much.

With so many Tomaszowers struggling to make a living, luxuries were rare. Many of our day-to-day activities were accomplished in a relatively old-fashioned manner for the late 1930s, when conveniences of modern living had already been introduced in larger cities and more advanced countries. Because our building at Antoniego 21 did not have running water for drinking, cooking, and bathing, we had to go to the pump in the backyard to fill pails with water and carry them into the house, which at least was more accessible than the services of a *wassen trager*. Pumping the water took skill. Marysia, our housekeeper and my nanny, placed the pail under the spout of the well, raised the handle, and with a few short strokes downward the water started flowing out of the spout. Mama heated the water on the stove and poured it into a metal tub. Then she washed me with soap, rinsed, and dried me with a terry-cloth towel.

Every few weeks, on a regular basis, a washerwoman came to our house. Franciszka was a short, stout woman in her early fifties, with light-brown hair combed away from her face, who wore a white blouse, a long, wide skirt, and a white apron of equal length over the skirt. We had an accumulation of clothing and linen, enough that Franciszka spent several days washing it. She used a large wooden washtub, a washboard, and brown soap. The washtub sat upon a wooden stand reaching her waist so she did not have to stoop as she scrubbed against the washboard. She fetched the water from the well in the yard, heated it on the stove in the kitchen, and lugged it to the attic. There, Franciszka would wash the laundry, starch it, and add blue color to brighten the white clothing and linens, then use a roller wringer to squeeze out water from the clean clothing and finally hang each item on clotheslines strung throughout the attic. Romek and I watched her work, while we played hide-and-seek behind the long sheets and duvet covers that served as ideal hiding spots. The attic was fun, and we took full advantage, playing games, running around, and chasing each other among the hanging linens and garments.

Outside I also enjoyed whatever fun a young child could discover. On holidays, parades would pass down our street and through town. There were soldiers dressed in uniforms, a detachment of artillery on horses, clowns, and marching bands. One day I joined the group of people walking behind the parade. Aunt Ruchel (Rachel) Jung-Cwilich, who lived on the other side of town, *iber der brik*, saw me walking and brought me back to my parents, who were looking for me.

The other parades in Tomaszow were Polish funerals, which were very elaborate. The casket was set on a shining black carriage, pulled by a pair of horses covered in black satin cloths, with black tall plumes inserted onto a strap on top of their heads. In front of the procession strode a priest or other cleric carrying a cross, and behind the carriage walked the mourners, followed by a crowd of townspeople.

Almost every day Mama's Uncle Avrum Jung came to our house. He was very religious, a member of Poland's Aleksander Hasidic group, another major Hasidic movement, which was based in Aleksandrow Lodzki, a town known in Yiddish as "Aleksander." Occasionally Uncle Avrum went there to consult the sect's spiritual leader, the Aleksander rabbi. Uncle Avrum was also one of the official slaughterers for the town, paid by the community for killing cows as well as poultry. His nickname was "Avremele Shochet" (*shochet* means slaughterer in Hebrew). Once I walked into a neighbor's house as he was slaughtering a chicken, spilling its blood into the sink below.

When I was in the crib, he would bend over and ask me, "Rivkele di schlufst?" "Rivkele, are you asleep?" I would shut my eyes tightly, making believe I was fully asleep.

Our backyard was surrounded by a fence, above which were visible the top branches of two trees. After I was told the story of Adam and Eve and the snake that lured Eve to try the forbidden apple, I imagined the Garden of Eden being on the other side of the fence whenever I looked at those trees.

Adjacent to our building was a three-story apartment building. On the second story lived Dr. Berliner, an ear, nose, and throat specialist, with his son Jurek, a boy of about fourteen who did poorly in school. They sometimes came out on the balcony facing our backyard where in good weather some of our employees sat sewing by hand, because the workshop was quite crowded. There, Papa's tailors sometimes overheard Dr. Berliner admonish his son to study hard, otherwise he would be given out to a tailor for apprenticeship, rather than receive an education. (Dr. Berliner and his family perished in the Holocaust.)

Next door lived Rudele, who had a grocery store. Rudele was a diminutive lady, thin with black hair, shining eyes, and a friendly, elongated face. She worked very hard managing the store, along with her husband and teenage son.

Rudele's store was an enchanting place for a child. In big glass jars she displayed a large assortment of chocolates and candies that came in all colors of the rainbow and a wide variety of shapes. There were striped candies, wiggly candies, and checked candies. The fragrant chocolates were enveloped in colorful silver and gold wrappings. On the counter was a glass tray for change, and underneath it was a decal from a cigarette advertiser. The glass tray was partitioned in half, and on it I placed coins for my little purchases. All along the walls of the store stood open sacks with staples—coffee, barley, flour, sugar, and a wide assortment of dry beans. Pickles and herring sat in barrels.

During the summer, when blueberries were in season, Rudele baked blueberry turnovers. Their enticing fragrance perfumed the air, luring me into the store to purchase the delicious delicacies. The top crust shone with the golden glow of egg yolks that were brushed on top of the triangular pastry before baking, and inside they were packed with fresh blueberries. When we brought them into the house they were steaming hot. Rudele's turnovers were so yummy that I can still recall their rich taste and the deep blue color they left in my mouth and on my tongue.

Religious Life

Poland was slowly transitioning to the modern era. That was also true for Jewish religious observance. Some Jews, like Grandpa and Grandma, remained highly traditional in their practices, while others, largely members of the younger generation like my parents, were far less religious, living a more secular life, though we celebrated all the major holidays.

Pesach—Passover:

In the spring, before Passover, Pesach in Hebrew, we scrubbed our apartment clean for the holiday, a major undertaking. Everything was washed: Mama took the kitchen cabinets, tables, and chairs out to the backyard, scrubbed them using a brush, hot water, and soap, then rinsed them with fresh water. While the cabinets were drying outdoors, she cleaned the inside of the kitchen, including a thorough cleaning and koshering of the stove. Only then did she bring the cabinets back into the house. Mama koshered the pots and pans for Passover by scrubbing them, boiling water up to the rim of the pots, and then dropping in a red hot rock to complete the rabinically approved process. She took the cutlery and dishes reserved for Passover out of storage and placed them in the freshly cleaned cupboards lined with new paper and trimmed with new edging. Mama also cleaned all the other rooms in the house, and even hung our rugs outdoors, then beat them with a straw broom until not a speck of dust could be seen rising.

For the night of the *seder* (the festive dinner and recitation of the Jews' exodus from Egypt) we went to my grandparents' home.

Grandma Raizel set her big, long table with a gleaming white tablecloth, two silver candlesticks in the center, and red cut-crystal goblets adjacent to each plate. Near the candlesticks stood a blue crystal goblet filled with wine reserved especially for Elijah the Prophet.

The seder in Grandma Raizel and Grandpa Hersh's house lasted well into the night so I slept over. My bed was near the window in the living room where Grandma Raizel had put up wallpaper showing peasants in red and blue outfits working in the field, cutting, gathering, and loading hay into wagons.

Sukkot:

For the holiday of Sukkot (the Jewish celebration of the harvest), my grandparents made a *sukkah,* (a temporary outdoor structure in which Jews eat during the holiday), which I helped to decorate with chains of white-and-blue paper that I made in school. We also hung on the sukkah walls pictures that Romek and I drew, and we covered the roof with branches of greenery.

Simchat Torah:

On Simchat Torah (the celebration of the annual completion of the reading of the Torah), we went to the synagogue, where children received a flag with a red apple stuck on top of the stick to which the paper flag was attached. The flag was very pretty, illustrated with a picture of the Torah ark, with its doors wide open, revealing the initials of the Ten Commandments. Waving our flags, Romek and I marched around the synagogue following congregants dancing with the Torah.

The High Holidays—Rosh Hashanah and Yom Kippur:

The one religious observance I absolutely dreaded was *kapores*: to rid one of his or her sins in preparation for Yom Kippur (the Day of Atonement) a live chicken was swung around and around the head so that one's sins could be symbolically transferred to the sacrificial chicken. I cowered as the squawking chicken hovered above me, frightened both for the chicken and myself.

Another tradition compensated somewhat for kapores—receiving new clothing to wear for the Jewish New Year, Rosh Hashanah, a practice my parents took seriously since they were tailors. One year for Rosh Hashanah my parents bought identical navy-blue rain capes for Romek and me. I remember how proudly we walked to our grandparents' house to show them our new capes. I knew they were a luxury item, and I felt very privileged to wear such a fine rain cape. It was manufactured of lightly rubberized fabric that made a swishing noise when you moved your hands across it. From the cape I could stick my hands out through the arm slits or keep them in the pocket of the coat that I was wearing underneath.

The following year my parents made identical great coats for Romek and me. They were wool, lined with rabbit fur, which made them very warm. Romek's coat was gray, and mine was tan. With the high leather black boots that our cousin Pola Margulies brought for us from Radom, we were both stylish and warm in our outfits.[4]

Jewish religious life in Tomaszow during the week revolved around the *Beis Midrash* (house of study) on Jerozolimska Street, and various *shtibels*—small synagogues.

Observant Jews would pray at the Beis Midrash or some of the shtibels, which typically were located in someone's house. Some shtibels had formal names, such as Chevrei Tehilim (the community of psalms); others were simply known by the name of the rabbi.

Avram Baitel's shtibel was the prayer house for Uncle Jozef and about thirty other congregants. Baitel ran the shtibel while his wife supported the family by raising and slaughtering geese.

Orthodox congregations, such as the Baitel shtibel, were often opposed to Zionism, which was a rapidly growing force in Poland, especially among the young.

"They were against Israel. They were so orthodox, it came Simhas Torah and they [the younger people in town] sang *Hatikvah* [which would become Israel's national anthem]. The older people said to the younger people, 'You're delinquents!'" recalled Uncle Jozef.

The fact that a sizeable number of Tomaszow's Jews were modernizing was clear at the town's biggest synagogue, the Groys (large) Shul on Handlova Street, where many of Tomaszow's Jews would attend services. The synagogue's leader was Rabbi Shmuel Brot, who was deeply involved in politics as a member of the Sejm, the House of Deputies of Poland's Congress, and a leader of the Mizrahi Zionist organization. Rabbi Brot would celebrate not just Jewish holidays, but Polish ones as well.

"The children in school used to march, and you'd see this rabbi coming to march also to give honor to the Polish holiday, and he'd

Groys Shul, Tomaszow-Mazowiecki. Courtesy of Tomaszow-Mazowiecki Yizkor Book.

come dressed in a top hat," remembered Fishel Samelson. "We'd come back to the synagogue, he'd come on to the pulpit and make a speech in Polish which was unheard of."

The Jewish community never lacked for controversy. At the Beis Midrash Avram Shmuel Romanowitz was a *gabai*, the man in charge of assigning synagogue service honors such as reading and carrying the Torah.

"When it came Saturday and they got the *aliyas* [honor to sing the blessing for a Torah portion reading], he always picked the poor people for the best honors, and the people who were rich came over and said to him, one of them said, 'Ve shayets' ['You're an outlaw']. Why you give the big honor to poor people?" said Fishel.

Within families, too, there were tensions over religious observance. The older generation often was strictly observant of Jewish practice, while the younger generation was more secular.

When the time arrived late in the day for *mincha/maariv*, the afternoon/evening prayers, Szmul Szampaner's father, Naphtali, would stop the horses pulling his soda delivery wagon so he could *daven* (pray) whether on the road or in the middle of a field. Eleven-year-old Szmul, who worked with his father, would stand and watch. When Szmul turned seventeen and joined an adult soccer team in an organized league, he would regularly play on Sabbath rather than observe the full day of rest with his parents.

"Sure I wanted to play; I belonged to the team. They said don't ask [your parents]," remembered Szmul. "[My] parents were mad at me."

Some Tomaszowers worked on the Sabbath because their employers required it, and still others violated the Jewish prohibition of working on Shabbes but did their best to hide the fact from the older generation. My father permitted employees to work in his shop on Saturdays. But when Grandma and Grandpa visited, they knew to put their work away.

"We were sitting around playing cards," recalled Srulek Rozanski. "The grandparents probably knew."

Lighting a cigarette on the Sabbath is also forbidden by a strict interpretation of Jewish law. But Srulek's sister, Genia Rozanski, remembered teenage friends sneaking a cigarette.

"People, they wanted to smoke a cigarette. They wouldn't smoke in front [of their homes so that] you should see. Saturday, to smoke a cigarette you would get a *patsh* [a slap]," said Genia. "My brother Liebel, he lit a cigarette, I'm sure."

Aunt Eva's relationship with her parents (my grandparents) was a perfect example of the generational divide between traditional parents and their teenagers who participated in Zionist or socialist youth organizations. She rebelled against Grandma and Grandpa's strict orthodoxy.

"Mother was very religious, even more religious than Father. When I finished elementary school, I rebelled because my mother was too strict," remembered Eva.

Her attendance at one meeting of the Bund (the socialist Jewish labor guild, which was entirely secular and nonreligious) led to a severe confrontation with her parents that she never forgot.

> Yankel Patz—he was a big leader in the Bund—he gave a speech, and it was very interesting. And my mother instigate[d] to tell my father I was there, to come and to take me home. My father came dressed like a Hassidic man. So one of my friends was sitting near me, and he said, "Chavale"—my Jewish name was Chavale—"your father is coming." He spotted [me] right away when he walked in.

> So I ran out. The only time in my life when I came home my father beat me. [Normally] my father never raised a hand. But my mother instigate[d].[5]

While many teens remained respectful of their elders' religious preferences even as they quietly rejected such orthodoxy, a few openly flaunted their independence from Judaism.

Fishel Samelson recalled Yom Kippur, a day of fasting, at the Groys Shul:

> I had a whole bunch of friends that davened in this shul. I used to sing in the choir. When it came to a part in the davening, they used to go out on the streets. Their big thing was to show that they are advanced and not religious. They would go to a restaurant while the davening was going on. So they'd go into a restaurant and in addition to that they'd order a hamburger [that was not kosher].
>
> There was a joke going around the holidays where this man, the owner of the restaurant, would meet sometimes on the street the father of this boy who went to this restaurant on Yom Kippur. And he would say to him, "Say, mister, can you tell me what is that holiday that a young boy is allowed to come in [and] eat an unkosher hamburger?"

But at home strict religious observance was the norm in many Tomaszow households. To comply with the prohibition against lighting a fire on the Sabbath, Jews would hire Poles, so-called "*Shabbes goys*," to do it for the price—paid in advance—of twenty grosz plus a piece of challah at the time of lighting.

Grandma and Grandpa were meticulous in their observance of the Sabbath prohibition against work.

"On Saturday I couldn't wash even my face. My mother didn't sweep the floor," marveled Aunt Eva. "It was unbelievable."

Grandma prepared well in advance for Shabbes. On Wednesday she purchased provisions for Sabbath dinner, including flour, sugar, oil, and eggs. Aunt Eva remembered Grandma Raizel making dough, letting it rise, dividing it into three pieces then rolling and twisting it to create braided challahs, then staying up late Thursday night to bake the challahs and cook soup.

Antoniego Street, Tomaszow-Mazowiecki. Courtesy of Tomaszow-Mazowiecki Yizkor Book.

"On Friday when she returned from the market she heated it all up [for the Shabbes meal]," said Eva.

At our house each Sabbath was a festive day. In addition to baking challahs, Mama prepared gefilte fish, noodle squares with lima beans, chicken soup, and boiled chicken followed by apple cake.

Shabbes lunch, after the morning prayer service, was an event as well. In preparation, on Friday afternoon Tomaszowers brought their pots of cholent (an Eastern European stew of beans, vegetables, and meat) to bakeries where they would cook overnight. Wealthier families could afford to fill their pots with plenty of meat, while those who were struggling often had none, at least when they dropped their pots off. Some, hoping for a better lunch, would make a quick switch when they picked up the cholent on Saturday afternoon.

"The poor people noticed what kind of pot the rich people's servant had put in. And when it came time to take the cholent, they took the rich people's cholent!" said Uncle Jozef.

Culture and Social Life

Antoniego Street was Tomaszow's social center on Saturdays following lunch.

"Saturday everybody went for a *shpatzir* [Yiddish for 'a stroll'].

Z.T.G.S. Jewish Sports Organization, football team. (Szmul Szampaner is seventh from left). Courtesy of Tomaszow-Mazowiecki Yizkor Book.

Young people would be dressed and promenade on Antoniego," recalled Genia Rozanski.

"The youth were dressed up and romancing, you know how it was with young people flirting," said Uncle Jozef. "Everyone was greeting each other with smiles. We talked, told stories, it was so lively. Young people lived with hopes things are going to get better. The whole week they worked hard and Saturday they lived it up."

Residents of Lodz would travel to Tomaszow, paying two zlotys for the bus ride, to enjoy Rode Park as well as the white-sand beach along the Pilica River, which was crowded by the afternoon.

On Saturday nights during the summer, there were dances on the beach. Jewish teens, though, might find trouble there. So they usually went to the beach in groups—for protection from Polish hoodlums.

While Tomaszow was a modest-sized community, its Jews boasted a particularly vibrant athletic, cultural, and social life.

Football (soccer), of course, was the sport of choice and the dominant team was Z.T.G.S., led by its star left guard, Szmul Szampaner.

"This was the best time in my life," recalled Szmul. "I was interested in sports, only sports."

Z.T.G.S. (pronounced in Polish by the letters *Zeh-Te-Geh-S*) was

Z.T.G.S. Jewish Sports Organization, cycling team. Courtesy of Tomaszow-Mazowiecki Yizkor Book.

the center of life for many of Tomaszow's young Jewish athletes. In Polish it stands for "Zydowke Towazystwo Sportowe," which means "Jewish Sports Organization."

The "C" league in which Z.T.G.S. played had a broad range of football clubs, including Victoria, a team of Volksdeutchen, (literally "folk Germans," native Germans living in Poland); various teams of native Poles; as well as Ha Koach ("the Strength"), an all-male Jewish sports club, and MLOT ("Hammer"), a communist team composed mainly of Jews.

Joining a company-sponsored team was a good way to gain employment. Shia (Stephan) Rajzbaum played for the Wilanow football club, which helped him land a job as a mechanic at the silk factory.

"It was like a push," said Rajzbaum. "That's why the young people had an attraction to the sports; they could help themselves with a job."

Another popular club sport in Tomaszow was cycling, and here too Szmul Szampaner excelled, once winning first place in the Tomaszow-to-Lodz fifty-kilometer race. Szampaner's brother Leibish specialized in calisthenics, where he was an award winner.

Jewish Orchestra, 1930, Tomaszow-Mazowiecki. Courtesy of Tomaszow-Mazowiecki Yizkor Book.

Off the athletic field, chess was a club specialty. School children would participate in live, life-size chess matches, moving around a giant chessboard as pawns, rooks, knights, king, and queen.

Z.T.G.S., though, was more than a sports-and-games club; it was a social organization as well, sponsoring Saturday night dances known as "Fives"—since they started at five o'clock. For just one zloty Tomaszowers could dance to a live band, but at that bargain price there were no refreshments at the Fives, just music and dancing.

In 1939, only months before World War II started, Z.T.G.S. even sponsored a children's summer camp where sixty boys and girls enjoyed sports and social activities.

"We spent a beautiful summer in camp," said Fishel Samelson.

Z.T.G.S. also had an orchestra. Fishel played clarinet, but poor technique cut his musical career short.

"I used to study at home, the clarinet. Not being able to use it the proper way, I used to get terrible headaches. . . . You have to know how to blow the instruments, and I was overdoing it," admitted Fishel. "My mother made me give it up."

When they had money to spare, Tomaszowers could visit one of the movie theaters in town. One zloty was the price of admission to the Odeon or the Modern, which both featured the latest Polish films as well as American movies, including cartoons and Shirley Temple movies. Aunt Eva, a big moviegoer, used her connections at the theater to get two or three tickets for the price of one.

On the second floor of the Modern movie theater was Tomaszow's casino, where the town's wealthier residents played cards and other games of chance. The impresario, a man by the name of Bernstein, earned good money from his enterprise, but he was known as a very stingy person.

Tomaszow had numerous live performances. Ha Zamir (The Singer) was the local Jewish musical group; Jewish and Christian children sang together in another choir; and a children's mandolin orchestra was directed by Tomasz Krulikowski (who would later be killed in Auschwitz).[6] There were also two amateur theater troupes sponsored by political and labor organizations. The Bund staged shows at its office, while the Zionist group Poalei Zion performed at one of the movie houses. Among the Jewish-themed shows they staged in Tomaszow were "Mechirat Yoseph" ("The Selling of Joseph") and "Bar Kochbar," who was the legendary leader of the Jewish revolt against the Romans during the second century in ancient Israel.

"My mother used to take us to the theater, and when I came back I used to sing the songs; I sang all the songs from the theater," recalled Aunt Eva, who occasionally performed her repertoire at one of the local butcher shops upon the proprietor's request.

While Tomaszow lacked its own professional Jewish theater, Yiddish companies from larger cities as well as the United States would tour through town, bringing big stars of the Yiddish stage like Miriam Kressyn to our local theaters.

Tomaszow's two competing weekly Yiddish newspapers, *Tomaszower Wochenblat* (Tomaszow's Weekly Paper), edited by Nuta Goldkrants, and *Di Shtime* (The Voice), whose editor was Beno Kurtz, reported on the cultural events as well as social, political, and business developments and even carried items about Tomaszowers who had emigrated.

Politics

Cultural diversions helped Tomazowers take their minds off the problems of the day, which were plentiful. Not only was the econo-

Gordonia Zionist Youth Group. Courtesy of Tomaszow-Mazowiecki Yizkor Book.

my stagnant and jobs scarce in the mid-1930s, but a severe brand of anti-Semitic hatred was spreading.

In the face of virulent anti-Semitism, though, Poland's Jews, including those in Tomaszow, failed to respond with a unified voice. They split along political, economic, and religious lines, placing hope in very different answers to their common problems. There were political disagreements over language—Yiddish (favored by the orthodox) versus Hebrew (favored by Zionists) versus Polish (used by modern families like ours); religion—observant versus secular; and response to anti-Semitism—build a stronger, more just Jewish society in Poland (which the Bund advocated) versus emigration to Palestine (the Zionist solution).

These various political movements grew rapidly due to the troubles of Poland's Jews. The Bund was the largest Jewish political organization. With an estimated 100,000 members in the mid-1930s and strong representation in Tomaszow, it was Poland's dominant Jewish labor federation, seeking to address the problems of Polish Jewry by promoting a socialist vision to resolve economic inequities.

Beyond the Bund, Tomaszow's Jewish workers were united through five different guilds, for tailors, bakers, shoemakers, carpenters, and butchers. Only Jewish barbers shared a guild with non-Jews. The labor unions were quite active. In 1931, during a workers' protest at the Wilanow artificial-silk factory, more than eighty people were arrested, including Jews. And on May Day (May 1) leftists would demonstrate on the streets of Tomaszow.[7]

Zionist groups offered a different hope for Tomaszow's youth, promoting *aliyah*—emigration to Palestine, where they intended to rebuild a Jewish homeland. Among the Zionist youth groups organized in Tomaszow were socialist-leaning Ha Shomer Ha Tzair (The Young Guard), Ha Noar Ha Tzioni (The Zionistic Youth), Po'alei Zion (the Workers of Zion), Hitachdut (Confederation), Gordonia (named after A. D. Gordon, a leader of the Palestinian labor movement), as well as Betar (founded by Ze'ev Jabotinsky in Riga, Latvia) and Mizrahi (Eastern), a religiously orthodox faction of the World Zionist Organization.

Gordonia would host what it called "living newspaper" discussions on Saturday evenings. The organization encouraged members to move to Palestine to help build agricultural settlements there, which angered many parents in Tomaszow.[8, 9]

While Zionist youth groups promoted aliyah, the Yiddish cultural movement, led by the Folkspartei (the Yiddishist People's Party), was fiercely anti-Zionist, believing there was no need for Poland's Jews to leave their home.

Local Tomaszow politics centered around the Gemina, the Jewish Council, led by Boleslaw Szeps, a wealthy and charitable businessman who founded an orphans' home and served as its director.

Szeps receives high praise in the *Tomaszow Yizkor* (remembrance) book:

> The local industrialist Boleslaw Szeps took it upon himself to do for the masses more than for himself. When he started to show his intensive deeds, then Jewish Tomaszow saw a person who was different. He was not like the rich people who give a bone to a poor person.
>
> He put himself with his energy and his clear thought to do what was good for the community. He got the name "the father of the poor people."[10]

Boleslaw Szeps, industrialist, philanthropist, Gemina leader. Courtesy of Tomaszow-Mazowiecki Yizkor Book.

Szeps had a prominent front-row seat in the Groys Shul. From his position in the choir, Fishel Samelson saw Szeps whenever he attended synagogue.

"I used to face him. I remember the way he used to dress, excellent, with striped trousers and a vest; beautifully dressed," said Fishel.

Jews were integrated enough into Tomaszow's larger society that some were members of the city council. Tomaszowers even served in Poland's military. Among them, Avram Shmuel Romanowitz, who was a member of the cavalry, Nuta Romer, and Leibish and Szmul Szampaner, who were foot soldiers in the infantry.

Anti-Semitism

Even though Jews were actively engaged in Polish society, culturally, politically, even militarily, anti-Semitism was widespread in the country and Tomaszow was no exception. Through the 1930s, well before the Nazis overran Poland's border, Polish government officials attempted to restrict kosher ritual slaughter, encouraged boycotts of Jewish merchants, and condoned random acts of violence. Polish anti-Semitism was a flammable bias that had seeped into the country over many years. The Nazis merely had to ignite the fire that would consume Tomaszow's vibrant Jewish life.

Yes, Tomaszow's Jews dealt cooperatively with Poles on a daily basis, serving them as customers—Papa and Mama sewed for hundreds of gentile clients—and hiring them for domestic help—Marysia and Franciszka were indispensible to us. But, as close as our contact, the relationships were, after all, based on business. There were few pure friendships between Poles and Jews, in large part because of the underlying current of anti-Semitism, even among children.

"They would call you 'dirty Jew' or say 'go to Palestine,'" said Zlacia Warzecha, who recalled Polish kids hurling insults along with snowballs outside school in the sixth grade. "We were a little scared."

When Rose Reizbaum was a young girl, a Polish friend turned against her:

> I was walking to school and this girl from school was throwing stones at me, and I said, "Why are you throwing stones at me? What did I do to you?" And she said in Polish, "You dirty Jew." I said to her, "What are you talking?" And she said, "Go away. I don't want to talk to you, I don't want to be friends with you anymore, you dirty Jew.'"

Jewish boys heard taunts of "Zydek, Zydek" ("Jew, Jew") from their Polish contemporaries, who also called them "Mojżesz" ("Moses"). But when the abuse became physical, Szmul Szampaner and his friends would fight back.

"Coming home from the sports club a few times Polish children wanted to beat us up—about fifth grade. We beat them up too. We'd fight back. We'd win more of the fights; we'd chase them away," said Szmul.

Once, Szmul and his pals were confronted after a Z.T.G.S. exercise lesson in which they were using wooden rods.

"They were waiting for us when we went home from the exercise. We went out with [the rods]. We beat them up. They never came again," said Szmul. The Z.T.G.S. instructor had trained the group well.

Anti-Semitism was infused throughout Polish society. A daily newspaper published in Warsaw, *Gazeta Polska,* was dedicated to a boycott of Jewish businesses. On its masthead was the slogan, "Patronize Your Own."[11]

"There was one guy who used to distribute the paper, and used to openly scream 'Don't buy by Jews! Don't buy by Jews! Don't buy by Jews!'" recalled Fishel Samelson.

"There was a bakery; we knew the people they were neighbors of ours. Suddenly you see a sign that said 'Christian Bakery.' It was never before 'Christian Bakery,'" said Fishel.

As anti-Semitism spread, some Poles who were friendly with or employed Jews became nervous.

Rose Reizbaum's father worked for a Pole who owned real estate in Tomaszow. One day he told Rose's father—a deeply religious man—that he could employ him only if he altered his appearance so he wouldn't look so obviously Jewish, even offering him money to do so.

"He took out from his pockets a lot of money and he put it on the table, and he said, 'I want you back but under one condition, if you'll cut the beard, because I cannot have a Jew with a beard,'" recalled Rose.

> And my father looked at him, and to tell you the truth we would be very happy if my father listened to him cause this way my father would be more safe and second of all we need[ed] the money because this man helped us a lot. And my father looked at him and said, "You know what? I don't sell myself on money. . . . I will never take it off even if they come and try to take it off and I won't cover it and I won't take your money! Take away the money if you want me to cut it off, I don't need your money!"
>
> So he puts the money back in his pocket, and closed the door with such a noise we thought the whole house would fall apart. . . . Then he said to my father, "You are a terrible Jew!"

Increasingly, anti-Semitism became official state policy. In 1937 Poland's Sejm and Senate passed a law placing restrictions on kosher ritual slaughter, a serious effort to curtail an essential practice of Jewish life, which made it more difficult but not impossible to purchase kosher meat.[12]

Though anti-Semitism confronted us each day and the decrees

that spread through Nazi Germany in the mid-1930s were worrisome, the Jews of Tomaszow, like those in other Polish communities, had no vision, no concept of what was about to befall us, no understanding of the potential depth of man's inhumanity against man.

Tatus thought of taking our family out of the country. He considered visiting the United States to see the World's Fair in 1939, but Mama, who was close to her parents, preferred to stay.

"He wanted to take the family and go to the U.S. He was a rich man; he had a successful business. But my sister didn't want to go," said Aunt Eva.

Once the war started, Mother did write to her Uncle Isaac Tenenbaum in Detroit about emigrating, but at that point it was impossible to get a visa, and many countries closed their borders to Jews trying to escape from Poland. We were stuck in Tomaszow with no way of leaving the country.

Left to right, Jozef Tenenbaum, Isaac Tenenbaum, Avram Chaim, and Hinda Margulies, August 15, 1933. Courtesy of Rena Margulies Chernoff.

2: Wartime in Tomaszow

World War II came to Tomaszow-Mazowiecki on a cool, cloudy, gray day—Friday, September 1, 1939—when Germany launched a surprise attack on Poland. Tomaszow was among the first cities targeted. Without warning at six o'clock in the morning, airplanes swept the skies overhead and unloaded their deadly bombs on several locations in town. The first victim was Mr. Leon Finer, an engineer who was known as "Engineer Finer" because in Tomaszow an engineer was addressed by his title, just as a doctor. He happened to have been standing on a balcony of his plywood factory at the time and was killed instantly. The Nazis would later take over Finer's factory.

On that first day of the war, Nuta Romer walked out to the street, seeing the German planes flying overhead. His neighbor Stephan Wojcichowski pointed and said, "Those are our planes!" Nuta responded, "We don't have planes here!" Since Poland was badly outnumbered and lacked modern fighter aircraft, the country presented no resistance to the German air assault on Tomaszow.

On day two a German plane dropped a bomb at the corner of Antoniego and Moscickiego Streets, destroying a bus terminal and a gas station.

Two days later, on September 4, 1939, there were heavy air attacks on the Wilanow textile factory.[1] We ran down to the cellar of our apartment building and sat on the basement floor, hoping to assure our safety, while some neighbors sat on the steps leading underground, allowing them to glance outside for a look at the attack. As we sat, a bomb damaged the house next door, number 19 Antoniego, home to the Rubinek family. Another bomb hit and destroyed a large apartment house down the street, at the corner of Ulica Palacowa.

We heard an announcement on the radio that all able men should go to Warsaw to defend the country against the foreign invader. Father, together with many other men from our town, left immediately for the capital to join the resistance effort. He boarded a bus where he met Uncle Jozef and his wife, Andzia, who was pregnant and expecting any day, as well as their daughter Fryda and Andzia's sister, Mania Warzecha.

They were traveling to a Warsaw hospital where a doctor would deliver the baby. Shortly after Andzia gave birth to a baby girl, Dorka—nicknamed "Bombowiec"—they had to go down to the hospital's bomb shelter, as the city was under attack.

Other people left Tomaszow by whatever means possible: buses, trains, cars, motorcycles, horse-pulled wagons, horseback, even by foot. While some, like my father, went to volunteer to help the military fight Germany, others were simply trying to escape the attack. Fishel Samelson, his father, two uncles, and a cousin placed some belongings on two bicycles and arrived in Warsaw in two days with the intent of continuing on to Russia. But they could go no farther since Warsaw was surrounded.

As people traveled toward Warsaw, German airplanes swooped down, bombing the roads and the fleeing masses. What ensued was panic. Every time a German plane flew low people tried to run from its aim, but they were not always successful. Many were injured or killed. The roads became clogged with corpses, dead horses, and destroyed vehicles, making the trip to Warsaw extremely difficult.

Mama, Romek, and I remained in Tomaszow because Grandpa said there was no use running away. Now that Father was gone it fell upon Mother's shoulders to manage the business.

In Warsaw my father stayed at the home of Aunt Pearl Golda and Uncle Moshe Torem, along with Uncle Jozef, Aunt Andzia, Fryda, and Cousin Mania. Because food was scarce people had to stand in long lines to get a loaf of bread.

"It was no food, no water. So we had to go to the Vistula River [to get water]," said Uncle Jozef. "There were a lot of horses lying in the streets shot by the Germans. People cut pieces of the horses, dead horses . . . and that's what they ate."

"I also ate at one time horsemeat," confirmed Fishel Samelson, who spent four weeks in Warsaw. "My father was able to get a big chunk of meat from a dead horse."

Tatus, Uncle Jozef, Uncle Moshe, and his son Jakub Torem traveled east from Warsaw as part of the defense campaign. However, they went only a short distance before the quickly advancing German Army unfurled its might, forcing them to return to Warsaw. The capital capitulated, and Poland surrendered to Germany on September 28, 1939. Soon after, Father and other Tomaszowers returned to town. Others remained active in the resistance effort, including Cousin Jakub Torem, who served as an underground courier during the German occupation. We never heard from him afterwards, though, so I believe he was caught and murdered.

Wehrmacht soldiers (armed forces) marched into Tomaszow on September 6, the sixth day of Germany's invasion. Volksdeutschen, the local ethnic Germans who lived in Tomaszow, gave a warm welcome to the Wehrmacht, standing on the sidewalks, cheering troops as they marched through the streets, waving their flags—red with a white circle and a black swastika planted right in the center of the circle.

The janitor of our building was a Volksdeutsch. He had a shortwave radio in his apartment so he knew exactly what was happening. As the Germans marched into town our emboldened janitor embraced the soldiers, even donning a German military uniform. Unknown to us, he had been a German spy, which we learned only after the soldiers had arrived.

Other Volksdeutchen also joined the Germans, including a man by the name of Kemp, who worked next to Shia Rajzbaum in the Wilanow factory.

"Two weeks before the war broke out, this guy disappeared, didn't show up for work, and we couldn't figure out," recalled Shia. "And the first [time] German soldiers came into town, he came in a Gestapo (German secret state police) uniform."

Wearing German uniforms suddenly gave Tomaszow's Volksdeutschen—our neighbors—a sense of authority and entitlement, recalled Shia, to the point that they began confiscating personal property of the Jews.

"You have a free hand; you can take whatever you want. Everything belongs to you was their attitude," said Shia. "The uniform made them feel so important."

Before long, the Nazis gave formal permission to Volksdeutschen to abuse Jews and confiscate their property. One local Volksdeutsch traveled around town with his horse and wagon. When he located an item of value he desired, he'd simply arrange to receive a permission slip from the German authorities and then claim the property.

The German soldiers immediately put Jewish men to work, cleaning up the ruins of bombed-out buildings and removing corpses from the streets.

One day I was sitting at the open window of our apartment, which faced the main street. A German soldier with high black boots, dressed in a green uniform, happened to walk by and started to talk to me. I called over my mother, and he asked her whether she was Jewish.

"Sind Sie ein Jude?"

Mother answered in German that indeed she was Jewish.

The soldier continued, "Wenn Sie ein Jude sind, dann wird es für Sie sehr schlimm sein," meaning, "If you are Jewish then it will be very bad for you."

We did not understand what he meant by "bad." We had held a positive opinion of Germans, especially since Germany was a cultured nation, a country of poets and musicians. Tomaszowers also recalled good experiences with Germans during World War I, when they had treated the population better than the Russians had. So "bad" did not have any concrete meaning for us. But it soon would.

New regulations and restrictions were posted around town. Among the first orders: young men were required to register with the German authorities. Some were sent to a work camp in Belzec. Others like Josef Zamulewicz were sent to another labor camp in Lublin.

"They kept us in a camp [where we] made air landing strips for the Germans," said Josef, who later escaped and returned to Tomaszow.

On September 8, Wehrmacht soldiers began robbing Jewish retailers. They shattered windows, marched into stores, then denuded them of all goods.

"First the Wehrmacht came in. Then the Gestapo came," said Srulek Rozanski. "They ripped open a big Jewish store on Jerozolimska Street, cigars, tobacco. The Germans ripped open the door, and they right away took all the merchandise."

Young German soldiers, guns at the ready, entered a shoe store where Rose Reizbaum worked and grabbed whatever merchandise they desired. They appropriated leather from shoemaker Zyndl Samelson, Fishel's father.

"The Germans decided we'll take the whole thing away. And they did," said Fishel.

The Gestapo handed over Jewish-owned businesses to Volksdeutchen, including textile factories belonging to Mr. Bornstein, Mr. Aronson, and others. Small stores still under Jewish ownership had to display a sign: "Juden Geschäft" ["Jewish-owned store."]

Rosh Hashanah, the Jewish New Year, arrived five days later. That afternoon as Jews through town were preparing for the holiday, German troops blocked off several main streets and began arresting Tomaszowers.

Rose Reizbaum was doing a favor for her brother-in-law. He had left his *tallis* (prayer shawl) at his parents' home and had asked Rose to retrieve it. Upon finding the tallis, she stepped outside to a scene of chaos. Tomaszowers were racing about, trying to evade the troops. Rose sprinted to a building where friends of her father resided. They quickly pushed her behind a partition before two German soldiers entered.

"Did someone come in here? I saw someone come in here!" barked one of the soldiers. Her father's contacts covered up, insisting no one had entered. They were risking their lives to protect her. Later that day Rose was able to emerge and returned home to find her mother sobbing outside her house, fearing that Rose had been captured and shot.

When Srulek Rozanski saw troops blocking his street, he hid by ducking into the stairwell of an apartment building. But when he stepped out black-uniformed SS—Schutzstaffel—guards arrested him. (Schutzstaffel were feared Nazi elite guards who perpetrated many Holocaust crimes.)

Srulek's sister Genia watched the SS capture her brother along with other Tomaszowers.

"They were in the middle of the street, Prezydenta Moscickiego, running," said Genia, describing the roundup. "'Schneller!' the troops screamed. 'Schneller, schneller' (faster, faster)."

Srulek was one of 200 people arrested that day. The SS forced their prisoners into three trucks, which then drove for three days to Czestochowa, Poland.

"We were split into groups of 100. Then they sent us to Göerlitz, a POW camp (a prisoner-of-war transit camp for Polish prisoners). We were there for eight days. Then the Germans said we were going home. I said, 'It doesn't look to me like we're going home.' They took us to the train and then sent us to Buchenwald," said Srulek.

It was to be a long, hard trip, beginning with a train ride to Rawicz, Poland. Once the Jews disembarked they were forced to run through two rows of German soldiers, who struck them with knotted rubber and leather whips. Some of the men succumbed and could not get up. Those that were able ran to waiting trucks, where they were required to hold their hands behind their necks. The trucks then brought them to the prison of Rawicz, where they were locked up, six men to a cell. The following day the Germans took them outside and distributed soup and a piece of bread. In the afternoon the soldiers put the prisoners back into the train, which traveled through the day and into the night, arriving the next morning at Weimar, Germany, a city located ten miles from the Buchenwald concentration camp.

After parading the Jews through Weimar, the German soldiers ordered their prisoners to raise their hands and run the full ten miles to Buchenwald beating them with guns and whips as they ran. Many fell and were killed on the spot. Of the ninety-one Tomaszowers that were taken to Weimar only thirteen survived.[2]

"They didn't care for anybody," said Srulek.

The survivors, Srulek among them, arrived in Buchenwald on October 15, 1939, the first transport of Polish Jews to be sent to the camp, where they would spend most of the war.

In Buchenwald Srulek was stripped of his personal possessions, including the apprentice contract that he had from my father. They were stored in a safe, and at the end of the war, Srulek was able to retrieve them.

Though imprisoned, the Tomaszowers were permitted to write letters home every two weeks. Srulek wrote, "Dear Parents, Sister and Brother, I feel very good but please send me money." (Zlotys were always helpful for bribing camp guards or obtaining extra food.)

"We were so happy that at least someone writes that they are still alive. We didn't know they're alive," remembered his sister Genia.

"Everyone came to our house to look on this letter. They said if one lives maybe the others live too."

In response, Genia would rush to the post office to mail a letter with some silver zlotys. My father, who had employed Srulek, continued paying his salary to the family and sent him additional money as well.

Srulek was assigned a variety of jobs in Buchenwald. Eventually, he was able to move into bricklaying, working with non-Jews on the construction team, a stable position that allowed him to survive the war.

Father's employees Chemja Tenenbaum and Szmil Rozenberg also were arrested in Tomaszow at the start of the war, but Mama was able to arrange their release. The German officers Von Bismark and Kurcakowski had come into Tomaszow and asked, "Who is the best tailor in town?" The two officers, wanting custom suits made to order for themselves, were led to our workshop. Mother informed them that if they released Chemja and Szmil, the two prisoners would sew the suits for them. Von Bismark and Kurcakowski confiscated fabric from the stores owned by Mr. Rubinek and Mr. Brzoza, Mother cut it, and once Chemja and Szmil were released, they sewed the suits for the two officers.

When Father returned from Warsaw he made several suits and a leather coat for Kurcakowski. The German soldier was very grateful to my father and since he knew what was in store for the Jews, he offered to take our immediate family—Father, Mother, Romek and me—to Switzerland in his airplane. Father refused Kurcakowski's generous offer, not knowing what was to come. Besides, my father had Hanka and Rutka in our household, and he thought that, no matter what, he would be able to save and protect them, as well as our immediate family.

School Ends

Once the war broke out, the Nazis did not allow Jewish children to go to school. The Jewish gymnasium (high school) and the public elementary schools for Jewish children, including Mrs. Zylberowa's, which I had attended, were shut down and would not open again.

At first a private tutor taught me Hebrew and *chumash* (bible) in the house, but that soon stopped. After a while the *melamed* (teacher) did not come to our house any more because it was becoming too dangerous for him to teach children. So I went to another private instructor, Mr. Meldung, who taught me Hebrew and chumash at his home. Some of it stuck; after the war the first Hebrew word that I remembered was "degel," which means flag.

Mr. Meldung was not far from our home, and I was allowed to walk there by myself. For lunch Mama had me take a sandwich of a roll with butter and sometimes cheese. Along the way a poor woman, Chavele Naar, meaning "Eva the fool" (though she was not so foolish) sat on a stoop at the entrance to the barber shop. Chavele Naar was a well-known town fixture. She wore a long, wide, flounced skirt reaching down to her ankles, and on top of it an apron, sometimes several aprons, a jacket, and a full scarf that covered her head and reached down to her back. Chavele spread out a kerchief before her on which she displayed candies for children to buy at prices below those in the candy store. Now that the war had begun her clientele and source of merchandise dwindled. That's why she was so glad to get my lunch. I was a poor eater and was happy to give away my sandwich to Chavele every day on the way to Mr. Meldung. Chavele appreciated my generosity and looked forward to my arrival and daily donation. Of course, I didn't tell my mother that I gave the sandwich to Chavele, so Mama was satisfied, believing that I ate well. Eventually, though, it became too dangerous to study at Mr. Meldung's. Chavele lost her free lunch, my formal education stopped completely, and I spent my days languishing.

Growing Restrictions and Terror

In October of 1939, the local Hitler Youth with the help of Volksdeutchen burned the Groys Shul on Handlowa Street to the ground. Within days they did the same to the Beis Midrash.[3]

The German authorities now forbade public worship, which led Jews to gather clandestinely in small groups to hold services. When the Germans barged into an apartment and caught Jews praying, they paraded the unfortunates through the street, still wearing their prayer shawls. Nazis spotting Jews with beards would use knives to chop off their facial hair with chunks of skin attached.

"It was terrible to see," remembered Shia Rajzbaum.

Grandfather Hersh had his beard torn off his face during such a brutal assault. This was an awful blow to Grandpa and our family.

German police cutting sidelocks of a Jew in Tomaszow. Reprinted by permission of Yad Vashem Photo Archive.

The beautiful white beard on Grandpa's face signified his dignity and his deep religious conviction. Now the nakedness of his face, exposed and injured, was not only a painful physical attack but also an assault on his sense of self, and by extension the entire family felt his pain. To quote from Holocaust scholar Daniel Landes, "This was a purposeful shaming. The Nazis knew how to assault one's self-dignity. To jeeringly pull the hair from the 'glory of a man's face,' the *hadrat panim* of his beard, was to serve notice, painfully, that this man no longer had a God to serve."[4] Some men covered their beards with scarves around the face, as if they had a toothache, to evade the enemy's wrath and avoid becoming victims.

More restrictions on Tomaszow's Jews soon followed. The Nazis imposed rations on food, limited the bakery's hours, and prevented the butcher from receiving deliveries of meat. Funerals for Jews were forbidden.

"My grandfather, Elimelech Samelson, died. We couldn't have a funeral," said Fishel Samelson. "We had to carry his casket through the side streets to the cemetery. We were looking for a space. We couldn't find a space. And, right in back of my uncle's monument there was a space. And we buried my grandfather there."

In October of 1939, the Gestapo declared a curfew. Posters across town announced that from 7 p.m. until 7 a.m. all Jews were to be indoors. Since Jews had to wait in line for bread in the morning that provided German forces with easy enforcement targets—people who got onto the bread lines early. Those who came before 7 a.m. would be shot.

Still, Tomaszowers were able to violate the curfew by traveling through each other's backyards, avoiding the main streets.

"You could walk from one end to the other," recalled Zlacia Warzecha. "You couldn't go across the street."

Boleslaw Szeps, president of the Gemina, urged people to save themselves by leaving Tomaszow as random terror became increasingly widespread.

Our family, like so many others, had the misfortune to suffer some of those fatal attacks. One day a Gestapo officer demanded that Cousin Hershel Tenenbaum hand over gold that he had been hiding. Hershel complied, but the officer killed him anyway.

In response, Hershel's older brother, Cousin Chemja Tenenbaum, who worked in my father's tailor shop, decided to leave Tomaszow with the intention to return as soon as the situation improved. Chemja drank a glass of wine with his parents and closest family, his father wished him good luck, and he took flight on November 12, 1939. As the German army advanced east, Chemja kept on the run, maintaining distance from the military. He was able to save himself, spending the war years in Russia. Afterwards he returned to Tomaszow where we met again.

That November a transport of Jews from Lodz came to Tomaszow, arriving with only the belongings they carried on their backs. This was one of the methods the Germans used to isolate and disorient Poland's Jews. People who had homes and extended families suddenly became homeless beggars in a strange town. It had a disquieting impact on Tomaszow's Jewish community, which was obliged to absorb, feed, and house them, as well as empathize with their traumatic experiences.

Then, on December 22, 1939, the Nazis made it compulsory for all Jews over six years old to wear a white armband with a blue

Chemja Tenenbaum (upper left), Hershel Tenenbaum (upper right), with their siblings and parents. Courtesy of Emmanuel Nefussi.

Magen David (Star of David) on the right upper arm, a so-called "Juden Zeichen" (German for "Jewish sign"). Jews caught without their armbands could be beaten or even shot on the spot.

This latest order impelled more young people to escape to Russia (most of whom survived the war). Binem Grossman, another of Papa's workers, was among those who left. Eventually he made aliya to Israel and settled in Haifa. Others wanted to leave Tomaszow, but ties to their families or businesses convinced them to stay.

The First Ghetto

The distinction between *iber der brik* and *in der gas* began to end in late 1940, when authorities mandated that all Jews living *iber der brik* had to move into town—by doubling up with those who lived *in der gas*. To compound crowding, the Nazis also required Jews who lived in surrounding, smaller towns to move in with Tomaszower households.

Yet another decree forbade Jews from living on the main streets of town and in the nicest sections, which forced us to move from Antoniego Street. Father found a small apartment on the second floor of number 3 Ulica Jerozolimska, apartment 5, where we moved on December 7, 1940, and would stay for a year.

It was a considerable inconvenience to move. We used a wagon and slowly transported most of the belongings, making multiple trips to bring as much as we could to the new apartment. My brother and I walked alongside the wagon, carrying the few toys that held the greatest importance to us. I carried the boat with the sailors, and Romek filled his arms with several balls.

The building on Jerozolimska Street was a three-story house. Like our prior residence and most apartments in Tomaszow, it had no running water so I had to fill pails with water from the pump in the yard. I would place the bucket under the spout and pull the handle several times up and down till the water started to pour. When it was stuck I would suspend myself from the handle, using all my weight to push it down. Sometimes adults were around the well so they would help me by adding a few pumps to my pail.

Our apartment on Jerozolimska was compact. At Ulica Antoniego we had six rooms. Now our residence was reduced to two rooms on the second floor facing the back. One room was a bedroom-kitchen combination, and the other served as a workshop, dining area, and a second bedroom. Since the Germans tried to confiscate all valuable possessions, we had to hide our bales of fabric and materials. In the workshop Papa built a false wall, behind which he stored some of our furs and fabrics. The remainder of our fabrics Papa wrapped in impregnable coverings and buried in the ground under the cellar of my grandparents' house at number 7 Bozniczna.

While the apartment was less convenient for our customers, it was still close to our former home on Antoniego (which was outside the newly created ghetto) and there was not yet strict enforcement between the boundaries of the ghetto, so some gentile clients still came to have Papa make their suits and coats.

One day a former employee of my father, Chamul Belzycki, who must have held a grudge over some issue, told the occupiers that Papa was hiding fabrics. Meister Hans Pichler, a thirty-year-old, tall, slim soldier, who walked very erect and looked over the heads of people rather than at them, came to our apartment and with a cane pounded on the walls until he heard a hollow sound. He ripped that wall open to find the hoard of fabrics and had a truck come to take it all away.

Implementation of the establishment of Tomaszow's ghetto fell to the Gemina, the Jewish Council, which under the Nazis would come to be known as the Judenrat and would be the means through which the Nazis communicated many of their edicts. Requiring Jews to enforce decrees was one of many Nazi techniques to pit Jews against each other.

The Germans selected the nine Judenrat members. Mr. Bernstein, an attorney before the war, was appointed chief of the council. Eventually he would be shot for disobeying a Gestapo order to submit a list of Jews to be killed. Mr. Ritchke, originally from Danzig, was appointed chief of the Jewish police (*Ordnungsdienst* in German, literally meaning "order service"). Ritchke, who spoke excellent German, eventually resigned after recognizing the reprehensible nature of the position and obtained a job as a helper to a German truck driver.

Bernstein, Ritchke, and other Judenrat leaders arranged for families with larger apartments to take in refugees from smaller towns and for Tomaszowers to make room by sharing apartments. Not only might a family have to move, but it also would have little say over who would be sharing its new home.

Uncle Jozef was required to trade apartments with a doctor who had a four-room apartment that the Judenrat ruled had to be split among four families, one room per family.

"It bothered me, but what could you do? You couldn't help it. You had to do it," said Uncle Jozef. "It was a complicated thing. You wanted to pick a family (you knew). You couldn't do it. You had to go to the Gemina and plead to put in a certain family. You had a hard job to get in friendly people. They would put in squealers sometimes. . . . Next to me, a neighbor of mine was a squealer [who would report to the *Gestapo*]."

Uncle Jozef, like my father, continued working out of his new apartment, creating garments for Poles as well as some of the occupiers who would enter with their German shepherds. Cousin Fryda, who before the war had been bitten by a police dog and had now witnessed dogs biting Jews in the ghetto, was terrified.

"I was lying there frozen with fear, unable to budge," said Fryda. "The dogs the Germans brought would come into this sleeping space, where I was told to go to sleep," remembered Fryda. "They were sniffing me. It was horribly scary."

There often was no electricity, so at night the Tenenbaums relied on a carbide lamp that emitted an unpleasant odor.

"I couldn't tolerate smelling that awful smell," said Fryda. "I guess my parents couldn't tolerate my fussiness. They told me to go in another room. The other rooms were dark and cold."

As Tomaszow received Jews the Germans had expelled from other cities, poverty and hunger in town became an acute problem. Before the war there was a public kitchen to assist Tomaszow's poor. But now the need grew exponentially. Mr. Bigeleisen, a Judenrat member, was in charge of organizing a ghetto soup kitchen, which at this point in the early stages of the war was financed by the American Joint Distribution Committee.[5] Outside financing helped but could aid only so much, particularly since it was extremely difficult to obtain produce for soup, forcing the kitchen staff to buy on the black market at highly inflated prices.

At first the Judenrat kitchen distributed 100 bowls of soup a day and a piece of bread with each serving. When the allocation from the Judenrat increased, it provided 300 bowls with bread, and eventually the kitchen was serving 1,500 meals a day.

The Judenrat, which had the power to arrest and jail those who refused to comply, called for contributions from wealthier people to help feed the poor. Even with additional help, the council was unable to prevent starvation.

Members of the Judenrat received favorable treatment from the Germans, more food and better living conditions, which created resentment among the rest of the population. But anger was greatest at the two dozen Jews who were members of the Jewish police unit that enforced Nazi demands.

The kindest of the Jewish police tried to show a bit of mercy.

"If somebody was supposed to get ten lashes, some policemen were counting one, two, four, six, eight, ten," said Zlacia Warzecha.

But other Jewish officers were particularly enthusiastic in their enforcements, as Zlacia learned when she received a whipping for staying home from her job at the local German workshop to care for her nieces, who were ill with the mumps. Jewish officers used leather whips to punish her.

"I thought they were going to kill me," said Zalcia. "I was black and blue for weeks, weeks."

Killings became part of Tomaszow's routine. The various Ger-

Jewish policeman with Jews in the ghetto. Reprinted by permission of Yad Vashem Photo Archive.

Jewish policeman with Jews in the ghetto. Reprinted by permission of Yad Vashem Photo Archive.

man authorities, including Gestapo and Schutzpolizei—uniformed police also called Schupo—would engage in random murders, frequently targeting intellectuals—doctors, teachers, writers. Sometimes at night they would round up victims and shoot them outside the ghetto walls. In the morning Jews walking to work were horrified to see friends or relatives dead, lying in the gutter. Later, police ordered workers to the cemetery to dig graves for the dead.

With no warning the occupiers would declare *Aktions*, roundups for the purpose of torturing or killing Jews. In May 1940 some Tomaszowers suspected of being communists were taken to be shot, then left on the streets for all to see. Soon after came the Jewelry Aktion, during which the German authorities demanded all kinds of valuables from Tomaszow's Jews.

"While we were standing in the roll call, they took out four people and shot them right in front of us. Then they said, 'Now you go home and bring everything that you have. If not, you're going to be shot now.' So, we were so scared," said Uncle Jozef. "We stood around a light-colored blanket and people threw their jewelry onto it." As Uncle Jozef watched he could think of only one thing—the blouse his daughter Fryda was wearing held family jewels in clandestine pockets he had sewn into the garment's shoulders.

"I was so afraid I ripped the shoulders open. I took it out and I gave it away. Everything that I had I was so afraid that they're going to search. They couldn't search, but how could you know? They just picked up one person, and they found him, they would shoot him. And we lived with fear," said Uncle Jozef.

The Jewelry Aktion was frightful for Fishel Samelson as well, who also had used his tailoring skill to hide a family heirloom.

> I had sewn in a gold chain that belonged to my mother. Years ago when a young couple got married, instead of buying a diamond, you used to buy a chain, a gold chain. I remember it was a very heavy chain and it had a little gold picture underneath on the end of the chain.
>
> I sewed this chain into my shoulder [of my jacket]. When they gathered all the people— and what happened they wanted to scare the people. I saw what was happening, and here I still have this piece of gold and I didn't give it in yet. I was scared something will happen. So I went over to an officer, a German officer, and asked

> him if he'll allow me to go into my house, which was twenty feet away, and my intention was to get into the house, take off this jacket, put on another jacket, and come down.
>
> As I was in the house, this guy Bettich came after with me with his gun. And he said, "What are you doing here?" And I said, "I had permission to come up into my room. I thought maybe by chance I had left something silver, something metal." And I gathered a few spoons that were lying around. And I thought he was going to take out the gun and shoot me.
>
> The minute I got down back to the group, my cousin was shot. My cousin was one of the four people that was shot by the Gestapo on that day in order to scare the people to give up their valuables.
>
> But here I still have the jacket on. . . . I still have the gold thing in my jacket, standing in the group. And suddenly my youngest sister, was at the other end of the group, comes over to me and said, "Did you give back the gold chain already?" And when the people standing next to me heard that I still have a gold chain, they all wanted to kill me because it was, if they find the gold they'd shoot us all. And I don't know where I got the strength, but I took my jacket off and I grabbed the sleeve of the jacket, and I just yanked it, and I tore the sleeve off. As I did that a Gestapo man walks over to me, he was a young guy, he was the shortest guy of the Gestapo, and he said to me in German, "What do you have here?" I said, "Well, I still have a piece of gold here, and I forgot to give it in, and I wanted to give it in." So he put it in his pocket and he walked away.

Such Aktions were among the most dramatic events foretelling the growing danger that was to come. But there were other indications as well.

In the late summer of 1940, an emaciated man in a ragged coat was sitting on a stool, leaning against the wall of a house. He was voraciously eating a slice of dry bread that someone had given him. He used his finger to spread his snot on top of the bread. There was a group of about twenty people surrounding him, including me. We looked in disbelief at his appearance of utter depravity. He told of hunger and death and unbearable conditions in ghettos in various towns through which he had traveled. We did not believe him; we thought he was spinning tales. Not in our wildest dreams could we picture conditions being so horrific, imagine the heartlessness and brutality of the German occupier. I had a feeling that this man came on a self-imposed mission to warn us, because he did not stay in Tomaszow but moved on.

That summer on *Tisha B'Av* (a Jewish day of mourning in memory of the destruction of the Great Temple in Jerusalem on the ninth day of the Hebrew month of Av), Jewish men between the ages of fourteen and forty had to register for work. Some, including Szimszon Koszerowski, a leader of the Bund, were sent to forced-labor camps in Lublin and from there to Cieszanow. Many of these men died in the labor camps. Others Jews in Tomaszow were put to work in the River Wolburka, where they had to carry heavy rocks, walking knee-deep in the flowing water as guards beat them with wooden clubs and rubber rods.

Workshops

To further their war effort, the Nazis in 1940 established slave-labor workshops. In Tomaszow those Jews who had a skill that the Nazis could use were put to work: tailors, shoemakers, watchmakers, carpenters, and printers. There was even a slipper factory, as well as a laundry. The purpose was to cater to the needs of the German soldiers stationed in Tomaszow and the surrounding area.

"One day the Germans came to confiscate my sewing machine," remembered Uncle Jozef. "My wife complained, 'How will we make a living?' The German said, 'You'll be thankful to me that he'll be working for the Germans.'"

Tailors were in demand for sewing uniforms, as well as nonmilitary clothing for the occupying Germans, who merely had to go into a workshop and order whatever apparel they desired. Non-Jewish Polish citizens could take advantage of the Jewish workers' services, but they had to pay a fee, which Gestapo officers pocketed. Each master tailor worked with a group of assistants to sew the uniforms or suits. My father's staff included Aunt Eva, Uncle Meylekh, cousin Chana-Fraidel, and several others. Jakub Wolard had his group of tailors, as did Uncle Jozef. For their labor the tailors received a half-loaf of round, dark bread every Saturday, some margarine, and a potato.

"There were about 100 tailors. I had seven, eight people work-

Jews lined up for the march to the Tomaszow ghetto workshop. Reprinted by permission of Yad Vashem Photo Archive.

ing for me," said Jozef. "Those people working in the shop got a labor card. We worked six days, Saturday only half a day. Private Germans had a right to come up and order things (clothing). Since I was known in the city and I had a lot of clients, so they came up and brought me some bread, some sugar to survive."

The workshop was located in a converted mill, on Moscickiego Street, in town but outside of the ghetto. On the bottom floor were carpenters. The second floor had tailors in a large room: about twenty different "shops" or teams of tailors. This was known as the Schneiderei, the tailor workshop. At the far end of the room were several fitting rooms. Upstairs on the third floor were shoemakers. And on the top flight dressmakers designed and produced clothing for wives of Gestapo officers who were now living in Tomaszow. Sometimes they also made dresses for female Volksdeutschen.

Each day workers would line up in the ghetto and wait as Jewish police counted them. Then they were marched to the workshop.

"If the armband wasn't perfect, you would get a beating from the Jewish police," recalled Genia Rozanski, who was a seamstress.

Father continued his business on the side so he could provide additional support for the family, employing Avrum Gersztein to work in our apartment at number 3 Ulica Jerozolimska. But eventually the arrangement caused us grief.

One day in the summer of 1940, Meister Bettich came to our apartment and requested that Papa sew a suit for him, free of charge. Bettich, who had followed Fishel into his home during the Jewelry Aktion, was a plump Volksdeutsch in his forties who was known as a troublemaker, even when he was a child. Not only did Bettich want Papa to do the tailoring at home after a full day at the workshop, but he wanted him to use his own fabric. My mother advised Bettich to go to the shop and order the suit there since that was where Papa worked full-time. Bettich looked around the partition in the room and saw Avrum Gersztein working at a sewing machine. "What is this?" he exclaimed. After that Bettich sought revenge. He went to the workshop and ordered a uniform to be tailored by my father. When it was done Bettich claimed that a cuff on the sleeve had a cut, and that this was an act of sabotage. Papa was arrested and imprisoned in the Tomaszow jail.

I was completely beside myself, crying bitter tears that such an act of injustice should befall my father. Romek also was distraught. Under these circumstances a person was guilty with no ability to defend himself, rather than innocent unless proven guilty. I thought that when I grew up I would like to be a lawyer to defend people from unjust accusations. I know for certain Papa did not cut the cuff on the sleeve. It may have been a baseless claim on the part of Bettich to impose his will, or some worker may have made a cut inadvertently, and here was my innocent father forced to pay for this alleged offense. My mother pled to the German authorities and to Bettich for my father's release, but to no avail.

To make matters worse, Papa was transferred from the prison in Tomaszow to a larger one in Piotrkow, a more secure facility. Now Mama had to travel to Piotrkow to see Papa. She was able to stay with a Tomaszow native, who lived in back of the Piotrkow jail during the war.

Mama wanted Papa released at any cost so she gave money to Uncle Jozef's brother-in-law, a former neighbor of Bettich, to bribe him. The scheme worked. Tatus was released from jail, and we were delighted when he finally returned home.

Meanwhile, the Germans' cruelty only increased. One day, Mr.

Zelig Lask, who was working in the tailor shop, received his weekly portion of half a loaf of bread for the full week's work. Mr. Lask was heading to the public bathhouse to bathe himself. On the way he saw his son Moshe-Mendel returning from the bathhouse and gave the bread to his son. For handing off this half-loaf of bread, Mr. Lask was beaten badly by the Germans!

In spite of such abuse, it became clear to Tomaszowers that the Jews working in the shops provided value to the Germans and therefore stood a better chance of survival. So those in the workshops did what they could to get their families employed. Uncle Jozef used connections to get Nazi officials to bring his sisters-in-law, Zlacia and Frymcia Warzecha, into the shop at the end of September 1941. Zlacia knew nothing of tailoring, but Jozef taught her how to make lapels for men's suits.

"Uncle Jozef took me up into the shop. I didn't know then how to push a needle with the thimble. But I learned. If you want to survive you do anything that you could," remembered Zlacia.

In order to assure Rutka and Hanka's survival, Papa was influential in getting them work outside the shops. For Rutka he secured a position in the slipper factory (the Ditch), making slippers for German war invalids, while for Hanka he arranged a job working in the Wäscherei, or laundry, where she washed clothing for the German soldiers and cleaned uniforms returned from the front.

Hanka, now twenty-one years old, was of marriageable age, so Papa introduced her to his tailor Avrum Gersztein. Papa asked whether she liked him. Hanka answered in the affirmative, and soon he arranged for them to marry in the fall of 1941. As part of the dowry, Papa made several suits for Avrum. Hanka now moved from our apartment at number 3 Jerozolimska to an apartment on Handlowa Street to be with her new husband.

Other Tomaszowers were able to gain life-preserving jobs outside of the shops. Leibish Szampaner feared for his life because his team of tailors in the workshop was failing to produce their required quota.

"The workers were starving and couldn't work well," said Leibish. "A German soldier said, 'I'll shoot you, that your shop can't make the quota.'"

So Leibish ran off to a nearby town, where he was able to survive by quietly tailoring for Poles. Eventually he was recruited to manufacture black uniforms for Ukrainian guards and later made his way to Lodz, where he worked for three and a half years for a prominent tailor making clothing for a German officer who provided their sustenance.

"We split it. We had plenty to eat," said Leibish.[6]

Leibish's brother, Szmul, worked for an SS general, delivering gasoline to the front. He was able to return home once a week to bring food for his wife and child.

Sala Kenigsztejn worked for the family of a German officer in the criminal police force, cooking, cleaning, even dressing his crippled wife.

"I got no pay, like a slave," remembered Sala. "But I got food. . . . That's how we were alive. They keep us 'cause they need the people. When you don't work, then they shoot you."

It was these jobs, outside and inside the workshops, that would save the lives of a select group of Tomaszow's Jews.

Starvation

The half-loaf of bread that Schneiderei workers received each Saturday was not nearly enough to sustain them.

"Half-baked and it was wet," remembered Genia Rozanski. "And the rest you had to smuggle. If you wanted to have something, you had to run out from the ghetto and smuggle." To gain sustenance for their families, children and teenagers tried to smuggle out of the ghetto anything they could trade or sell.

"You risked your life to sell it. How many (times) I put here something to sell for a piece of bread? I would take a towel, a tablecloth to sell. Once I walked two miles to look for bread. People didn't want to sell," said Genia.

When we lived at Ulica Jerozolimska, Tomaszow was still an "open" ghetto. This meant that even though we had to wear the white armband with a blue Star of David, it was still possible for people to sneak out of the ghetto by surreptitiously lowering their armband from the upper right arm and carrying a sweater or other item over the arm to conceal the band, allowing some, particularly those who did not look stereotypically Jewish, to go beyond the boundaries, do business outside, and then attempt to bring provisions back into the ghetto.

Since many Tomaszowers did not receive even a weekly food

ration, workshop employees were sometimes confronted with terrible ethical dilemmas, as Josef Zamulewicz experienced:

> Saturday we used to work till twelve. When we went home from the tailor shop, they'd give us a piece of bread, a small piece of bread; we should survive until Monday morning.
>
> When I came into the ghetto my whole family was standing over there with the hands stretched out, and everybody begged for the piece of bread. Naturally I couldn't give them away, I needed it for myself and for my mother and for my sister. So this picture that I remember in front of my eyes, my whole family was standing and everybody was begging for the piece of bread. This I can never forget and I can never forgive myself that I could not help them with this piece of bread. I don't think there's anybody in the world, a writer in the world can write the feeling that I still have today about this moment that I could not share with them the piece of bread that I had. There's not a painter in the world who could paint a picture like this, the way my whole closest family stays in front of me, begging for the piece of bread, and I could do nothing. If I would give it away, I wouldn't survive to Monday morning. Even my mother wouldn't survive till Monday morning.
>
> Closest family—my aunt, my grandpas. They were standing, begging for the piece of bread, and I couldn't do it. I have such a feeling about it. Every time I think about it, it's impossible to believe. I feel guilt and not guilt. If you would give it away, you wouldn't survive. It's a terrible feeling.
>
> This feeling is something. All my life I'm going to have this, and I can't get rid of it. But this picture doesn't leave my mind and doesn't leave my conscience and I can't forget about it. Even today I cannot forget about it.[7]

Working for local Volksdeutschen, who would pay in food, became commonplace. In return for receiving tailored clothing some Volksdeutschen would smuggle in butter, eggs, potatoes, even ham, which most starving Tomaszowers who had consumed only kosher food before the war, didn't hesitate to eat.

Those who were not employed in the workshops attempted to find work through the *Arbeitsamt*, the German employment office. But such jobs were temporary, lasting one or two days, occasionally longer. The director of the Arbeitsamt was Mr. Reichmann, a local Volksdeutsch. A short, bald man, Reichmann was in charge of supplying Jewish workers to all German authorities: the Gestapo, the SS, the army, and sometimes even to German civilians. He was known for performing his duties in a very business-like, professional manner, without abusive behavior toward Jews.

Reichmann proved helpful to Wolf Kaiser, whose family was among those ordered to move to Tomaszow from Lodz. The family, like most, was starving, including his sister's two-year-old baby. The Kaisers had smuggled a collection of new socks from Lodz and knew they had to be sold to gain food, but selling on the black market was dangerous. Kaiser, who regularly sought work from the labor office, decided to try selling to Reichmann, and anxiously inquired.

> In the office Mr. Reichmann closed the door and invited Wolf to sit down. They were alone. Mr. Reichmann asked, "What is it?" Wolf fearfully said, "Sir, please forgive me. I have this problem. You see, when we came from Lodz to Tomaszow-Mazowiecki we brought with us some stockings, men's stockings, that is, of various kinds. Some are knee-high, with beautiful designs. I must sell them. We have no food in the house, and the baby is hungry. Could you, sir, need stockings? It would be good if I could exchange them for food. Also, I would like to thank you for the good jobs you are sending me to." Mr. Reichmann after a while said, "O.K. Bring some in and I will see if I like them; maybe I will buy them from you."
>
> The next day Wolf brought six pair of men's stockings, hidden in his clothes. Mr. Reichmann liked them and asked how much they cost. "Well, these days money is not worth much," said Wolf, "especially when one has to buy food on the black market. If possible, food would do well. Please, Mr. Reichmann, you decide what to give me for them." He knew well what Wolf meant. "Good," he said. "Leave it to me."
>
> For a few weeks Mr. Reichmann was more than generous. Every day Wolf smuggled socks into his office, and in return the German supplied Wolf with food and money. In Wolf's house for a time there was food again. But it did not last for long. Soon there were no more socks to sell. With the German, no socks, no food; and hunger returned to the family.[8]

Tomaszow ghetto. Courtesy of Tomaszow-Mazowiecki Yizkor Book.

Not everyone starved, though. Fishel Samelson's family was relatively well off because he, his father, and two sisters all had jobs in the workshop: Fishel was a tailor, his two sisters were seamstresses, and his father a shoemaker.

"We were considered one of the richest people at that time. For what were we the richest people?" asked Fishel. "My father, myself, and my two sisters, each one got . . . bread. You know what it meant in those years?"

"There were some people who walked home, they had four or five people in the house, and only one of them was working. . . . And each one was waiting already for that piece of bread. You know, we were rich with four. . . . It was unheard of."

On December 8, 1941, Tomaszow's ghetto was closed. This meant that Jews could not leave the perimeter without special permits, enforced under punishment of death. Anyone caught outside without official permission was subject to shooting by German soldiers.

As the ghetto was shuttered the Gestapo simultaneously reduced food rations so that people got only three pounds of bread a month, exacerbating their oppression.

To make matters even worse, supplies for the public kitchen that the Judenrat had organized were dwindling. There was a tremendous need for food but no way for the public kitchen to satisfy the starving population, so eventually the Judenrat shut its doors.

When the Germans closed the ghetto, they also further shrank its size, placing our home at Jerozolimska Street outside the ghetto's diminished perimeter. The Gemina required us to leave the apartment immediately so we moved to one room on Ulica Kramarska, on the second floor, where we stayed for only a brief period of time.

The Nazi restrictions forbade us to even look out upon the Aryan neighborhood, forcing us to cover with black fabric the aparment's windows that faced outside the ghetto. Life was free beyond the ghetto; people walked unencumbered on the sidewalks while here we were confined to a dark, cold room.

I caught whooping cough during our stay in the apartment and would cough uncontrollably. It came in spurts. To ease the coughing I drank warm liquids, and Mother made steam baths for me. She would heat a pot of water, then cover my head with a towel, and I would inhale the hot steam. She also was able to obtain some honey to try to assuage my cough.

Soon, Papa found a larger residence for us at number 6 Ulica Stolarska, apartment 1, where we moved on January 7, 1942, and would stay until September 1, 1942. It was a semi-detached, one-story house consisting of two rooms and a cellar with a garden in the back. Behind the garden was a wooden fence that was missing several slats. Looking though those gaps you could see the *boisko*, the local soccer field. In those days the boisko was abandoned; no one had an interest or mind to pay attention to sports.

We were in a situation fighting for our survival, fenced in a ghetto, prohibited from leaving its boundaries, completely cut off from the outside world physically, as well as intellectually, having no access to the printed page, the radio, or people beyond our communal prison. The Germans had confiscated all radios, and no newspapers reached us.

We were dependent on the meager servings of food that the Germans supplied, a starvation diet. Each person was given a ration card, and one was allowed only so much food per month. Indeed, many people died of hunger and disease. Josef Marshalik, the badhen from Aunt Eva's wedding, starved to death. My uncle, Avrum Jung, the ritual shochet, also died from starvation in the summer of 1942. He came to us a few days prior to his death and was lying in the shed in our garden, on a wooden shelf. We gave him whatever food we had, but he was beyond rescue. His body was emaciated and shrunken, and he died after a few days. He was taken by wagon to be buried in the Tomaszow cemetery. My aunt and uncle, Rachel

Jews in the Tomaszow ghetto. Courtesy of Tomaszow-Mazowiecki Yizkor Book.

Jews in the Tomaszow ghetto. Reprinted by permission of Yad Vashem Photo Archive.

and Szaja Cwilich, also perished from hunger in the ghetto, as did my Aunt Chaja and her husband, Uncle Avrum Szychter.

Aunt Chaja Szychter had been a wonderful housekeeper and chef. For a while she cooked meals for the SS men at their headquarters, which allowed her to eat well and also bring home some leftovers to feed her family. However, after some time she lost her position to a young woman and was forced to subsist only on inadequate rations from the Germans, which brought on her terrible hunger. Her daughter Simcha Bina, or "Sabinka," a beautiful little girl with dark eyes, black hair, and a shining complexion, could not look on as her parents and two brothers starved. One day she sneaked under the wires of the ghetto to get food from people on the outside. When Sabinka returned at dusk with food hidden inside her blouse, Johann Kropfisch, a German soldier who specialized in catching and killing Jewish children, saw my little cousin and shot her right in view of her mother, Aunt Chaja, who was waiting for her return inside the ghetto. Scenes like this were a common occurrence. In fact, Kropfisch killed hundreds of children. Simcha Bina's two brothers, Maier and Shlomo, were later deported to Treblinka, where they were killed.

The streets of the ghetto were filled with poor and hungry people. I remember them lying on the sidewalks stretched out, swollen from starvation, in the process of dying a terrible death. Some were dead already.

"Every day we found people who died from starvation. They covered them up with newspapers," remembered Aunt Eva.

A man with a wooden wagon pulled by a horse so thin that its ribs protruded went through the streets daily to pick up the bodies of those who had died the night before and bring them to the cemetery for burial.

"It was horrible. It was unbelievable, the way people suffered so much," said Eva.

Surrounded by starvation, my father saw the possibilities of that vacant lot, the boisko, and decided to plant potatoes there. The whole family helped out. First we fertilized the field with human manure, which was no problem with the outhouse in the backyard. Then we spaded the earth, made even rows with string, and planted the potatoes. We tended to the plants carefully, watering them, weeding the field, delicately using a hoe to gather earth around each plant as it grew. Leaves sprouted, then little white flowers bloomed. After a summer's wait each plant had several potatoes. In the garden that surrounded our house we planted carrots, cabbages, and beets. It was a rich harvest that we carefully collected and stored in the cellar.

We took two wooden barrels and grated the cabbage. Papa and Mama put boards on top of the cabbage and Romek and I climbed into the barrels and jumped up and down to squish it. The adults were too big to fit into the barrels, but Romek and I were just the right size for the job. The cabbage stayed in the barrels for a while till it became sauerkraut. Once we harvested the vegetables, Mama cooked huge pots of sauerkraut soup twice a week and ladled it out to hungry people who came to our door.

The garden also had a big cherry tree that yielded nice fruit. The cherries were picked very quickly, though, and there were not many left for me.

As Tomaszowers struggled to find food for survival, the shootings continued. On April 28, 1942, Gestapo troops arrived at Hershel Rozanski's home, ordering him to dress warmly.

"When he walked out of the house, they killed him. I remember the day," recalled his sister, Genia. "A cousin took me aside and told me, 'Hershel is dead.' . . . Later we saw him lying down, till they picked him up on Mala Street. Hershel's wife, Chana Rozanski, was arrested. We never saw her again. And we took in the children, two boys and one girl. We were heartbroken."

One night in May of 1942, I slept over at my grandparents' house at number 7 Buzniczna. I looked out through the window, and there in the yard lay the body of one of their neighbors, Cham Burech, a tall, fair-skinned redhead who lived in the adjacent apartment building. Blood was flowing from his head. The Germans had pulled him right out of bed, taken him outside and shot him. I saw a soldier still standing next to the body, his revolver in his hand. The Germans that night had forced a whole group of Jews out of bed and shot them, claiming they were communists. Once the German soldier left, people from the apartment house poured out to look at the corpse. They covered Cham Burech's body with a sheet, then removed the corpse to allow the *chevra kadisha* (burial society) to prepare it for burial at the Jewish cemetery.

That month members of the Judenrat, as well as Jewish doctors,

A murdered Jew on a Tomaszow street. Courtesy of Tomaszow-Mazowiecki Yizkor Book.

lawyers, and intelligentsia of the community, also were shot to death.

While some of Tomaszow's Poles and Volksdeutchen tried to help Jews they knew, others assisted the Gestapo in determining and locating their targets by spying on Jews. In return they received a healthy ration of food.

The killing, oppression, and starvation took a psychological toll and shook the foundation of our community's religious faith. Some practicing Jews stopped believing in God.

"Who wanted to believe? You heard all day, 'Nicht gut. Nicht gut' [No good. No good]," recalled Aunt Eva.

Yet some observant Jews maintained, "God will help." And, most Tomaszowers continued to believe that conditions could not get much worse.

"We were thinking that, after all, the Germans—it's a cultural folk. How could they?" recalled Eva. "We still believed maybe they will have a little conscience."

With the closing of the ghetto, no correspondence was permitted to the outside world—no mail, no telegrams. Still, some news trickled into the ghetto, as Machel Grossman wrote in Tomaszow's Yizkor book:

> The only persons able to go outside the town and into the villages and nearby townlets were holders of the "green armband." These were collectors of rags and leather merchants, who bought these materials from the local peasants and supplied them to the factories sequestered by the Germans. These "green armbands" brought news of deportations, removal of Jews from many townlets that were now "Judenrein" [rid of Jews], and continuous transports of deported Jews.
>
> But to where?
>
> No one knew. There were rumours that the deportees were sent to labour camps in Germany. The term "concentration camps" was also heard. If people ventured the supposition that the Jews were being taken to their deaths, not only did people turn a deaf ear to them, but they were also branded as madmen. Was it possible that young and healthy people without handicaps would be sent to their deaths?[9]

"How could you think that something like that could happen later on? Killing, gas chambers all these things," said Uncle Jozef.

"I was discussing with my father, my brother, maybe we should go to Russia too. . . . My father said, 'My age? I'm going to go now, leave everything? How will I survive? What will I do there?' We figured out another thing. They arrested the rich people and the educated people, doctors, lawyers. They put them into jail. We talked among ourselves. We are working people. We are not rich, why should they start with us? That's what we figured out. So we decided, my father and myself, we decided that we're going to stay, we're not going to go to Russia."

The Small Ghetto

In July 1942 the Gestapo began to separate Jews employed in the various workshops from the rest of the Jewish population, ordering those with jobs to move into an area bounded by the streets of Jerozolimska, Handlowa, Wschodnia, and Piekarska.

They enclosed the area with a barbed wire fence and a sentry box, where a guard stood at the entrance checking the working and identity papers of all those who entered what we called the small ghetto, a ghetto within a ghetto. There was a great panic as people tried to gain employment in order to be more useful to the Germans, believing that those in the small ghetto would be safe. Some tried to use bribes to get working papers, but the availability of jobs was very limited.

Soon after, we moved from Ulica Stolarska to number 11 Wschodnia, a former fish store, which was now a one-room apartment. Father, Mother, Romek, Rutka, and I all squeezed into the tight quarters, though we weren't the only ones who were cramped. Aunt Eva, Meylekh, and my grandparents lived in a two-room apartment with ten occupants.

About 16,000 Jews were crammed into both the small and large ghettos. Such congestion and poor sanitary conditions caused an epidemic of typhus fever. To make matters worse there were few medications.

The Jewish gymnasium (school) stood within the periphery of the large ghetto. Since the Germans had forbidden the education of Jewish children on any level, the building was converted to a hospital. But the Germans did not supply medications so the Jewish doctors on staff had to make do with whatever they could improvise.

As the winter of 1942 approached, the Nazis declared that Jews who owned furs had to bring them to the Judenrat, (now newly composed after the murder of the prior membership), which would hand them over to the Germans. The punishment for disregarding the order would be instant death. Mama, Aunt Eva, Romek, and I were confronted with a dilemma: we did not want to part with our furs, they were our possessions, and if we gave up our furs we would be helping the German war effort, allowing their soldiers on the front to benefit from the furs' warmth. But if we did not turn them in, we would be shot. We decided to make the best of the difficult demand by inconspicuously cutting the furs on the back of the skin, diminishing their value and utility to our oppressors.

When the Germans did not receive many furs, they started searching through Jewish homes and shot some people who had refused to comply.

At this point Tomaszow's Jews were so exhausted that resistance seemed impossible.

"You have to understand. We were so worn mentally that the only thing that you have to do is just to survive a day. For example, you saw a killing, you had to walk over the person. You couldn't do nothing. What could you do? We didn't have people in the ghetto who were organizers," said Josef Zamulewicz.

"How could you organize against such a power? Don't forget that the Germans killed 12 million Russians. And Russia was a power. It was very hard."

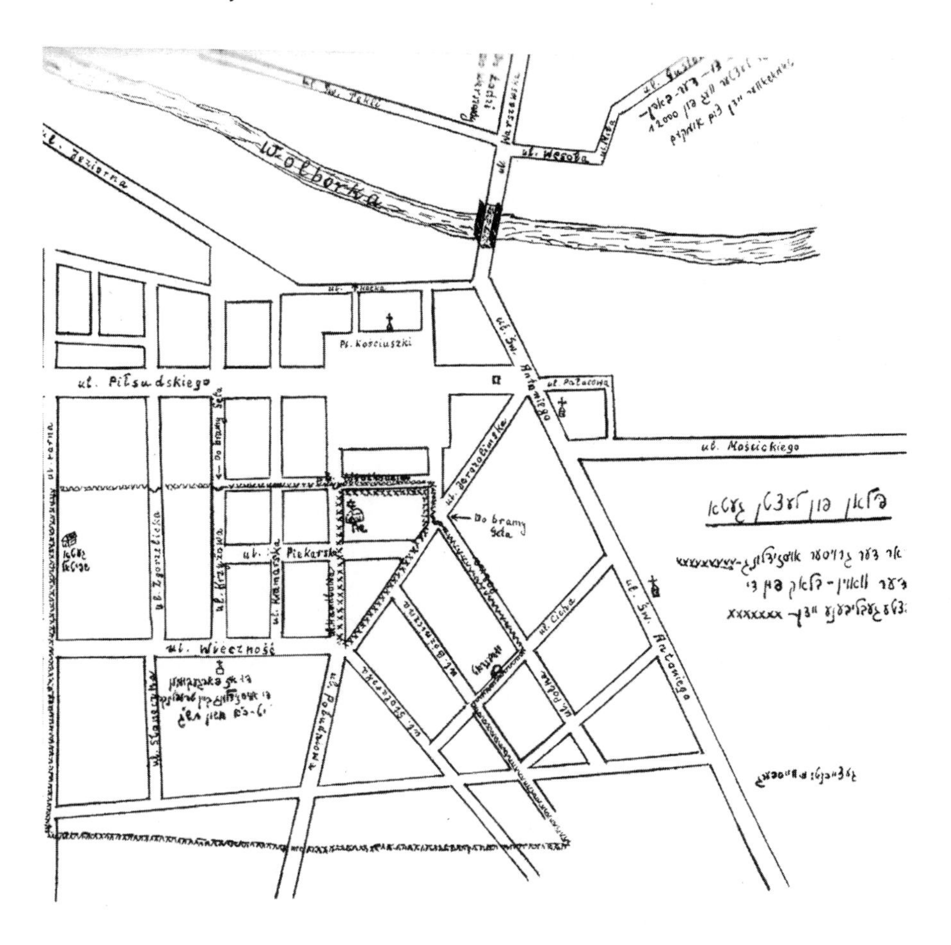

Map of Tomaszow ghetto and small ghetto. Courtesy of Tomaszow-Mazowiecki Yizkor Book.

3: Deportation

On Saturday, October 23, 1942, the Gestapo installed electric lights in the ghetto. A commission of several Gestapo and Schupo members arrived at the yard of the Jewish hospital, measured its dimensions and exchanged notes, but we did not know their intent.

There was a general mood of impending danger, a tension that everyone felt. At that time, Mama suggested placing Romek and me with a Polish family in return for all the valuables we still possessed. I do not know whether she had a specific person in mind, one of our customers or some other acquaintance. But I absolutely refused to be separated from my parents. The thought of living with strangers, with Poles on the Aryan side, was threatening to me. I was only nine years old, vulnerable and weak, and certainly did not feel strong enough to be able to protect my dear younger brother, Romek. Right away I told Mother that I refused to leave my family, I wouldn't be able to live. I'm sure I would not have been able to emotionally survive without my parents.

Sharing a fate with other Jews in a group, I always felt, would be less stressful than suffering as an individual, hiding alone with strangers. Since I was so determined in my choice, Mother and Father acquiesced to my wish so my brother and I remained in the ghetto with our parents. They probably themselves had doubts about leaving us with a Pole they likely didn't know well enough to completely trust, even though their motivation was to save our lives.

My decision was a wise one. Shortly after some of Tomaszow's Poles offered their homes as a place of refuge for Jewish people (in return for high compensation such as gold and jewelry), the German authorities announced that any Pole harboring a Jew would be punished, but those who handed over their secret boarders would be rewarded with food such as bread, margarine, sugar, and marmalade. Soon, most of the Poles in Tomaszow who had taken in Jews gave them up to the German authorities to receive extra food. Consequently, those Poles profited twice: once by receiving gold, silver, or jewels from the Jews they had pledged to help, and a second time getting extra food portions from the Germans. Not a bad deal for them!

There is no way of knowing whether I too would have been betrayed, but by staying with my family I felt secure, rather than worrying every second about my survival as I would have had I been with strangers.

On Wednesday evening, October 28, 1942, a contingent of Ukrainians in black uniforms armed with submachine guns surrounded the ghetto. The lights surrounding the ghetto were lit. Panic reigned. People tried to stay close to their dear ones, to huddle together and say good-bye because they feared something ominous was about to occur.

The Nazis announced that we would go to the "East" and would have to pay for our own transportation. This was typical of their deceptive tactics; they never told you the truth. And Tomaszow's Jews in their innocence could not foresee the cruelty and barbarism that awaited them.

Genia Rozanski went home to her parents, who lived outside the small ghetto, and told them she would be going with them.

"I was not supposed to be home," recalled Genia. "I said to my mother, 'I'm not going back. I want to go with you, my father, my mother, my brother.' She said, 'No, my child. You go. Maybe you can help us out.' I said, 'No, I'm not going. I want to go with you.' And she sort of pushed me. I remember even what she wore that time, a navy-blue dress with a pair of shoes I will never forget. And she pushed me to leave, and she said, 'Go, go my child. Maybe you will help us.' From the steps she was walking, I was walking, I said, 'No, Ma. I'm staying with you. How can you handle three grandchildren,' 'cause my brother wasn't alive. She said, 'Go, go. Maybe you will help us.' These were her words, her last words."

Then, on Saturday, October 31, 1942, the selection and deportation ("Aussiedlung" in German, "wysiedlenie" in Polish) began.

The Gestapo ordered all Jews who lived outside the small ghetto

Aussiedlung—Deportation of Tomaszow's Jews. Courtesy of Tomaszow-Mazowiecki Yizkor Book.

Patrolling Tomaszow during the Aussiedlung. Courtesy of Tomaszow-Mazowiecki Yizkor Book.

to pack clothing and leave their homes. Though we didn't know it, this was the deportation that would send most Jewish Tomaszowers to their death.

Street by street Jews were ordered to line up in rows of five and walk to the hospital grounds and then on to the railroad station. All those living outside the small ghetto where we resided were evacuated, from the area bound by the following streets: Jerozolimska, Polna, Cicha, Bozniczna, Poludniowa, Sloneczna, Graniczna, Stolarska, Lewa, and one side of Wiecznosc.

Anyone who disobeyed the order was shot immediately on the spot. People who were sick and could not move were shot in their beds. The Gestapo murdered about 250 Jews during the two days of deportation, as they forced residents to evacuate their homes.

Guards marched the Tomaszowers—men, women, and children—to the railroad station, where they confiscated their belongings, then crammed the prisoners into waiting cattle wagons. The Germans executed the evacuation with assembly-line efficiency. In all, 6,000 Jews were loaded onto trains that day and deported from town.

Monday, November 2, 1942, was the second day of deportation, targeting those of us in the small ghetto. That morning we were all very nervous. We knew neither what the day would bring, nor what our future would be.

The Gestapo, Schupo, and remaining Jewish police all participated in forcing families from their homes into the streets.

"When we went Monday the ghetto was almost empty. They told us to go in line, five people in a line and walk to the church," remembered Zlacia, who was wearing several dresses, two coats, and carrying as much clothing as she could in backpacks. "We walked on the street, Jerozolimska, then on Wieczna. I'll never forget the empty ghetto, open windows, the curtains were flying out. We saw dead people lying on the street."

We walked arms tightly entwined with our dear ones in our line, five in a row toward the hospital grounds, fearful of what would happen. In our row were Father, Mother, Romek, Rutka, and me. Behind us walked Grandmother Raizel Tenenbaum, Grandfather Hersh Tenenbaum, Hanka, and our two cousins from Warsaw, Zosia and Gucia Torem. Behind them were Uncle Jozef Tenenbaum,

Aunt Andzia Tenenbaum, their daughters Fryda and Dorka and Mania Warzecha.

The guards shot or beat anyone who fell out of line. Even the youngest, most innocent in the arms of their parents were not spared.

"Babies were dashed against the brick wall bordering the road and killed," remembered Fryda.

We walked toward the hospital grounds, until we arrived at the church on Wiecznosc Street. The church was an old wooden structure that also had a little cemetery on its grounds. At the gate to the churchyard stood the Gestapo Oberleutnant Weiser, who was in charge, and several other German soldiers.

Weiser selected who would go to the right, to wait in the churchyard, and who would be sent to the left— to a transport. Those with stamped working papers, who held jobs that provided the Germans with some benefit, he sent to the right. Those without he directed to the left.

Only a special connection could save those without working papers. As a prime tailor for the Germans, Papa had been assured that his family would be protected. But when the day of deportation arrived, a Gestapo officer instructed Papa to go to the workshop. Instead, he insisted on being present at the selection to try to save the family. Rather than going to the shop with Mama, he sent Aunt Eva and her husband Meylekh.

Father had obtained jobs for Hanka and Rutka. Now he hoped to shield other family members, as many as he could. He knew Weiser because he used to sew uniforms for him in the workshop. When our turn came before Weiser, Papa stepped forward and said, "This is my wife and children," and they let us into the churchyard.

Zlacia Warzecha and her sisters were right behind us. Zlacia had working papers, but her sister Mania did not. Papa was able to pass Mania off as his sister.

"How many are there in your family?" Zlacia recalled Gestapo chief Weiser questioning my father. "So he said, 'This is my sister, this is my brother.'"

He then tried to save Grandma and Grandpa, Raizel and Hershel Tenenbaum, telling Weiser, "These are my parents." But the German officer slapped my father on the face, snapping at him, "You have no more parents!"

My grandparents and the rest of our family, including Zosia and Gucia Torem, were sent to the left, forced to go to the hospital grounds, while we had to kneel in the churchyard.

Jakub Wolard, who worked near my father in the workshop, had a wife, Masha, and a son, Isaac, about my age. Weiser allowed Masha to go into the churchyard, but not the child, Isaac. Masha would not leave her son so she went with him to the hospital grounds for deportation, as Jakub watched helplessly.

Weiser split families with absolutely no compassion.

"First they called my father in," remembered Fishel Samelson. "My father walked in; they said, 'Turn. You go to the right.' My mother walked in; they said, 'You go to the left.' My grandmother went in, and she was holding her granddaughter, a six-year-old girl by the hand; they said, 'You go to the left.' Then my two sisters walked in, both to the right, then I walked in and go to the right, and that's how the selection was done, until the end of the people. Then the people they took in the left . . . they took them away. We didn't know where they were taking them."

German and Ukrainian soldiers forced those sent off to the left to the rail station, where they shoved them onto waiting trains, as Machel Grossman described in the Yizkor book:

> When it appeared impossible to pack more Jews into a wagon they were "assisted" with indescribable violence and cruelty by blows to the head of whips and rifle butts until the last one had been crammed inside.
>
> Such were the scenes of horror at Tomaszow station that day: families wrenched apart, children and parents searching frantically for one another. The Ukrainian butchers did not for a moment cease to belabour their victims. Nor did the Jewish policemen at the station escape their attention; they too were beaten mercilessly, rifle butts crushing their skulls, whereafter they were thrown into the wagons to share the final sufferings of their fellow-Jews.[1]

Those who lagged behind on the road, avoiding the selection, were then shot. Gestapo officers ordered Srulek Markowicz to take a horse and wagon and collect bodies of those who had been shot and take them to the cemetery.

Eight thousand Jews were deported from the Tomaszow ghetto and sent off on the trains that day. What had been a bustling community now seemed nearly abandoned. "In the houses hangs a silence that screams with unheard voices," wrote Grossman.[2]

Everyone was depressed. Everyone had lost family, friends, and acquaintances. No one could console anyone else because we all were in mourning. Mama wept from her heart for Grandma and Grandpa. We did not know where our dear ones went, what fate awaited them, but we knew that they had been mercilessly torn from us.

Some Jews who worked outside the ghetto met a Polish rail worker who told them that the deportees' final stop was Treblinka, where they were gassed to death and burned. No one believed that story because it was too preposterous, that live people should be murdered in such a ghastly and methodical manner. People thought that the peasant was an anti-Semite who had made up the story.

But confirmation came a few days later from Bolek Szteinman, whose wife and children were taken that day. He had been able to hide on top of one of the train cars and returned several days later, reporting that indeed our family, friends, neighbors, had gone to Treblinka, where they were killed and disposed of in the crematoria.

The Nazis deported, gassed, and burned approximately 14,000 Jews of Tomaszow in the crematoria of Treblinka. They took 6,000 Tomaszower Jews in the first deportation on October 30, 1942, and another 8,000 on November 2, 1942. Their ashes were among the more than 870,000 people the Germans massacred at Treblinka.[3]

Our family was destroyed. I lost my grandparents, many aunts, uncles, and cousins to the deportation. In all, about sixty members of my family, on both Mama and Papa's sides, were killed in Treblinka. We were left as a broken limb of a tree. The roots, trunk, and other branches were all gone.

It was due only to the fact that my father was a tailor in the workshop with some influence that our nuclear family and several other relatives survived.

There remained only about 750 Jews in Tomaszow-Mazowiecki, mainly workshop employees.

"It was like a cemetery. I remember the sound of the shoes, how they walked on the street. Was like a ghost town. You were afraid to look up," recalled Genia Rozanski.

I was acutely aware that I was among the few children left.

In a continuing campaign to hide their plans and prevent surviving Jews from knowing the truth, the Nazis had those transported to Treblinka write postcards, which were mailed to relatives remaining in Tomaszow. There was word that Masha Wolard had written to her husband Jakub, informing him that she was working on a farm in Germany with her son.

A few Tomaszowers took the cards as a sign that their deported relatives were still alive.

"No one could confirm whether it is true. So people deceived themselves, it was easier to believe, it made more sense," argued Machel Grossman.

But more Tomaszowers recognized that they would never see their loved ones ever again, that the Polish peasant and Bolek Szteinman had been right, particularly when hard evidence appeared.

The Germans ordered some of the remaining Jews to clean the homes of those who had been deported and bring anything of value to a huge warehouse, the *Sammelstelle* where Jewish workers, including Romek and me, sorted out the items: furniture, clothing, bedding, household goods, dishes, pots and pans, and silverware, all property of those who had been taken from us.

Romek and I worked in the china department, where we stacked plates, saucers, wine goblets, and vases, and put them into crates to be shipped to Germany. Every day we were confronted with the loss of our families and friends as we sorted their possessions.

Frieda Szajewicz was working at the Sammelstelle when she came across the rucksacks of her siblings and parents. She opened her brothers' bag and saw the shoes they had worn to the selection. At that moment she realized they had been sent to their death.

"Till then I thought they might have gone to work like the Germans said. But then I knew they had not," she said.

Fishel Samelson's family had a similar experience.

"Somehow my father got a job to work there [at the Sammelstelle]. And one day he came home and brought home my mother's shoes, my mother's coat, and my mother's dress, the one that she was dressed [in] when the selection was done. We knew."

We remained trapped in the small ghetto, squeezed in the cramped, one-room apartment with Rutka and Hanka, who rejoined us after her husband Avrum was deported. We all had to keep working as slave laborers for the Germans, Father sewing in the tailor workshop, Mother, Romek, and I stacking and packing items in the Sammelstelle, Rutka making slippers, and Hanka cleaning the Germans' clothing. After work I played hide-and-seek with Romek and several children that remained, or we just ran around in order to have some physical activity because all day we were confined in a small area in the Sammelstelle. I was glad to be with Romek and my parents, though we did not know what the future held for us.

Working in the Sammelstelle offered the opportunity to smuggle items out that could be traded for food. While I wasn't able to walk out with pieces of china, many of the older workers did remove items they were supposed to be packing for Germany.

"Sometimes I would take something and sell it to goyim [non-Jews] on the other side of the fence. I'd give a dress, shoes, then they would give me some bread," Frieda Szajewicz recalled. It was always bread that she would receive. "There was not enough to eat, but this gave us more."

"Our dream was to eat," she added. "They made it the only thing to think about. It's terrible to be starving."

We starved because the Gestapo provided only minimal rations at a soup kitchen: in the morning an ersatz coffee made from roasted barley and in the evening a watery soup, as well as a daily portion of bread, a little margarine, and occasionally a bit of marmalade.

The deportation and extermination of the majority of Tomaszow's Jews did nothing to ease the Gestapo torture of those who remained. Four months after the Aussiedlung, the Nazis killed off twenty of Tomaszow's remaining intelligentsia.

Then yet another deadly deception: the Palestine *Aktion*, a charade intended to offer Tomaszow's Jews false hope, which only resulted in more killings. One day people dressed in Red Cross uniforms arrived in town, announcing that they planned to bring Tomaszowers with family in Palestine to the Holy Land via Switzerland. All those interested should register.

Heated debates ensued. Is the offer genuine? Should we register? Should we stay?

"Some people said it's true," remembered Fishel Samelson. "Maybe. Maybe not. Some said it's a trick."

Papa and Uncle Jozef decided to register since they had family in Israel. The curfew was temporarily lifted so that those working during the day could register at night.

Tomaszowers struggled to recall the names of distant relatives who had made aliya to Palestine. The Germans then declared that friends and acquaintances would be adequate. Some Jews who still lacked connections to Palestine offered bribes to be added to the list.[4]

But just days before the "emigration," someone with connections to the Nazis found out it was a fraud. Papa and Uncle Jozef had their names taken off the list.

"We came back and told every family. So they knew already that something is wrong," said Uncle Jozef.

Some Tomaszowers who had paid money to get on the list now paid again to get off the list. But others were willing to take the chance, in spite of the Nazis' prior lies and brutality. Those on the final registry for Palestine assembled and boarded a horse-drawn wagon, which took them to the outskirts of town. There the hopeful emigrants were met with Nazi gunfire, shot to death. Just a few were able to escape and returned to Tomaszow to tell the story.

In March of 1943, in the Appell Platz (roll call place) between Piekarska and Handlowa Streets, the Nazis spread a blanket on the ground and assembled all inhabitants of the small ghetto around the blanket. At random they took out four people, Mr. Fainer, Mr. Platt, Mr. Wolkowicz, and Mr. Samelson (no relation to Fishel Samelson), and shot them. Then the Germans threatened, "This is what will happen to you unless you bring all your valuables and drop them on this sheet here." Fearing for their lives, the remaining Tomaszowers rushed to their apartments, retrieved whatever they still possessed, and dropped it on the blanket—watches, bracelets, earrings, rings, and necklaces, anything that contained gold or precious stones.

Yet another Aktion took place on the holiday of Purim, March 21, 1943, as described in the Tomaszow Yizkor book:

> A lorry drove up to the ghetto gate and cries of "Aufmachen ihr drekische Juden-schwein" ("Open up, filthy Jewish pigs") were heard. The speaker was Hans Alsch, a police officer, and he was quickly inside the ghetto. Through the main gate now appeared Hans Fichler (Meister of the "shop"), who at once presented the Jewish policemen with a list and told them that all the persons on it had to assemble at once, as they were to be sent to another labour camp.

A knock was heard on Dr. Mordkowicz' door (Mordkowicz was a well-regarded doctor who had still survived and had treated Oberleutnant Greiser for venereal disease), and the Jewish policeman Y.Sh.[5] entered, the list in his hand. From the list he reads out the names of Dr. Mordkowicz, his little daughter, his brother Menasze and his daughter, and he repeats Fichler's instructions. They must at once pack a few things, as they were being transferred to a camp, and the Germans were waiting for them.

In the meantime, other Jewish policemen were running here and there to round up the others on the list, amongst whom were fellow policemen. . . . Meister Fichler examines the list to see that no one is missing. When Dr. Mordkowicz arrives, holding his little daughter in one hand and his bundle in the other, he asks Fichler where they are going. Fichler burst out sarcastically: "*You are being sent to a place of rest.*" Little Krisza asks tearfully: "*Why do we have to be sent just today*?" for she had invited her friends to that very evening! "*Perhaps we could postpone our journey to tomorrow*?" Fichler placed his hand on her head, and she sensed it was the hand of a murderer and, wrenching herself free of him, clung tearfully to her father.

Meanwhile, everyone on the list had arrived, and they were loaded onto the lorry, with their baggage. There were 21 of them. When the lorry reached the house of Szeps, outside the ghetto, some armed gendarmes clambered onto it, among them the *Volksdeutschers* Fuchs, Walkowiak and Kropfisch, as well as *Gestapo* soldiers. In a car that followed sat Oberleutnant Greiser, Meister Fichler and Obermeister Siegert. . . . It was the latter who suggested that the Jewish policeman and his wife be included in the list, because he had seen him outside the ghetto accompanying a Jew to a dentist who lived outside the ghetto. For this "offence" the Jewish policeman and his family paid with their lives.

The procession proceeded to the cemetery. Helped by blows from rifle butts, the victims jumped from the lorry, which had stopped beside an open grave (to avoid attention this had been dug by Poles). At once, Fichler ordered the unfortunate Jews to take off their clothes. . . . Terrible cries then rang through the cemetery. Two women, Yazda Rejgrodska and her sister, refused, and one of them began to struggle with the murderers. . . . The two women now started to run screaming towards the fence. Krisza also burst

> into tears and began to make for the fence. Kropfisch, who was known for his sadistic trait of firing at the heads of small children, put a bullet into the head of little Krisza, and thus staunched her tears. The other butchers began firing at the Jews standing on the edge of the grave, while Hans Alsch, Fichler and Seigert ran after the two women—and a few revolver bullets halted their cries and their flight, whereupon the Germans said, *"Die verfluchten hunde haben die Kleider verseucht"* (*"The cursed dogs have ruined their dresses"*).
>
> Polish workmen filled in the graves. Afterwards, they said that the earth on top of the graves went on heaving for some time after the murders.
>
> Oberleutnant Greiser had remained in his car all the time, making sure that the murder of the 21 Jews was carried out punctiliously. The butchers, their hands and uniforms stained with the blood of their victims, climbed onto the lorry and returned to town, as did Fichler and Siegert in their car. Oberleutnant Greiser thanked the murderers in polite German tones for the loyal assignment they had carried out. This then was the "Purim gift" of the German butcher to the Jewish doctor who had cured him. Now his conscience was clear, for the Jew was dead—and thus Greiser was no longer obligated to him. Later that evening some soldiers and workers came to the cemetery to collect the clothes of the victims and take them to the store to be sorted.[6]

Around that time the Germans took all carpenters who were in the small ghetto and sent them to a camp called Blizyn. They were supposed to work on preparing barracks there, but that was all we knew.

On April 19, 1943, Jews in the Polish capital revolted against their captors. The Warsaw Ghetto uprising had repercussions in towns across Poland since the Nazis feared the spirit of revolt would spread. So, shortly afterwards, Ukrainian and Latvian guards wearing black uniforms with skull and crossbones on their caps surrounded Tomaszow's small ghetto. They would fire machine guns at anyone attempting to sneak out.

A few weeks later, on May 30, 1943, the Gestapo liquidated the small ghetto. The order came to take our belongings and evacuate our homes, so we brought as much clothing as possible, whatever we could wear. The Gestapo warned it would search all houses and apartments. Anyone found staying behind would be shot. Even so, a number of Tomaszowers remained, preferring to die in their homes rather than endure further torture on the way to what they expected would be an uncertain death. Indeed, Gestapo officers did find and kill them in their residences.

As we walked from the ghetto to the Tomaszow train station I thought, I will never see Tomaszow again. It was my hometown and I was sorry to leave it. But Tomaszow really no longer was a home for us; it had been destroyed by our enemies, the Nazis. Even now they surrounded us as we advanced toward the station. At least I was with my immediate family.

Only thirty-six people stayed behind to clean out the empty homes in Tomaszow. We felt sorry for them because we did not know what their future would be.[7]

4: Blizyn

The Gestapo packed us tightly into waiting train cars designed to transport animals—but now we were the cargo—about 120 people crammed together in each rail car. But because I was with my family it did not bother me. In all, they jammed 712 Tomaszowers onto the train.

It seemed as if we were en route for a long time. In fact, it was a journey of only fifty-seven miles to Blizyn, located in the Polish district of Radom.

Suddenly, the train stopped in the middle of a field. German and Ukrainian soldiers opened the doors and started yelling "RAUS! SCHNELL RAUS!" ("Out! Fast, out!"). While the soldiers yelled, they beat us with rifles and whips.

Since there were no steps we had to jump down from the high rail cars. As she landed Aunt Eva injured her knee and foot. Others also suffered injuries. Nevertheless, the soldiers forced us to run onto a meadow, and from there they led us to the camp gate where we lined up. The guards searched us, confiscating whatever few belongings we still had. Fishel Samelson, though, was able to get in with lots of clothing on his back.

"When we were brought in from Tomaszow to Blizyn, I must have had about a dozen shirts on me," said Fishel. "I had a jacket. I had an overcoat, I had scarves. Most of the people were frisked. I was able to get into Blizyn without anything taken away from me. In addition to that I don't know how much money I had sewn into my jacket. And I was able to go into the camp with all that. And little by little I used to sell that. I sell a shirt, I used to get two loaves of bread. An overcoat, I remember I had a brand new overcoat I had made in Tomaszow that I brought to Blizyn. God knows how many loaves of bread I got from a Polack at the wire, at the fence," said Fishel.

After the search the Nazis registered their prisoners, assigning us to barracks according to our work detail and separating men from women.

Until now we had lived as a family, Mama, Tatus, Romek, and I. But now Mama and I went to the women's barracks on one side of the camp, while Papa and Romek were ordered to the men's barracks on the other side.

Soon transports of Jews arrived from Piotrkow, Lublin, Radom, Bialystok, Kielce, and other towns and villages.

The camp's barracks contained three-tiered wooden planks that served as beds, seven prisoners to a slat, so that each person occupied only half a meter, as crammed as sardines in a tin.

Cousin Fryda was squeezed next to her sister in the bunk: "Every night as she lay beside me in our bunk, my little sister, Dorka, would sing herself to sleep. I loved hearing her, but sometimes I scolded her for not falling asleep sooner. I couldn't understand how she could be so happy and cheerful while so hungry, but what did a three-year-old who had been born into such conditions understand about cruelty in this world?"

Blizyn was an *Arbeitslager*, a slave labor camp; later on it would be designated as a concentration camp, run by the SS with many Ukrainian guards. While Blizyn was not designed as a Nazi death camp, many of our fellow prisoners would meet their death there, most frequently from disease, because the sanitary conditions were simply awful. Our barrack previously had been occupied by horses, so it was rampant with mice and rats. You had to cover your entire body with blankets to avoid the rodents. Twice, rats bit Aunt Eva on her nose and toe.

"Once at night at twelve o'clock, Busco, the assistant camp commander, came in and he woke us all, and he said, 'Out!,' recalled Aunt Eva. "It was snowing. I awoke and my nose was bleeding. I was bitten by a rat, and it hurt me very much, and I hardly could put on something. Everybody was out. I came the last one out. He said, 'Why did you come late? I'm going to give you twenty-five whips!' I said, 'Don't you see I was bitten by a rat. I couldn't get up. The rat didn't want to go away.' So he said, 'OK.'"

It wasn't only our barrack; the entire camp was infested with rodents. Screams punctuated the buildings at night as prisoners were bitten. Szmul Szampaner claimed some of the rats were the size of cats. "I throw the shoes at them, they wouldn't go away," recalled Szmul.

Zlacia and her bunkmates would place sheets on the plank above to prevent rodents from falling onto them. "We hung a sheet over a small piece of linen and at night, a whole day, we saw dancing the mice there inside," remembered Zlacia.

At night if we had to urinate we were forced to pee into a bowl, the same bowls from which we ate our soup.

The men's barracks used a different system, as Wolf Kaiser wrote:

> For a toilet, two huge barrels were put on each end of the barracks which were steady in use, because of the cold, and the amount of the people. The smell of urine was terrible. In the early morning, when the barracks were unlocked the barrels were removed by putting sticks through the handles of the barrels and two men . . . carried them out on their shoulders. After disposing of the contents, the barrels were brought back to put them in their place."[1]

Sometimes water was available from a metal pipe outside near the front of the barrack. Once, when the pipe had been dry for several days, Fryda recalled gaining permission to go to the nearby river to wash dishes.

"I remember passing the house where the commandant lived. I remember the most beautiful poppies in front of his house. The Ukrainian guards were cavorting in the river, jumping and swimming," said Fryda.

It was a stark contrast to our daily routine, which required hard labor of every person. Some were assigned to a loading and unloading commando; some worked in a quarry outside of camp, the Steinbruch, where they were breaking up stones; and still others were part of a road-building crew.

There was a very large shop as well. In a huge building that extended on and on, about 700 people worked in facilities for shoemakers, carpenters, knitters, blacksmiths, watchmakers, and, of course, tailors, all producing goods for the Wehrmacht, the German Army. The sewing machines and machinery for other trades were some of the very machines the Gestapo had appropriated from Jewish homes and businesses for the Tomaszow workshops; they had simply moved the slave labor production to Blizyn to continue benefiting from our efforts.

Each day at the tailor *Werkstatt* (workshop) Mother and I would reunite with Tatus and Romek. We were assigned to repair uniforms arriving from the front, as well as sew new, reversible uniforms for use in both winter and summer, green camouflage patterns on one side and white on the other for camouflage in the snow. Everyone had to complete a daily work quota, which I accomplished with Mama and Papa's help, sometimes at night. Using a special tool I made buttonholes, finished them by hand, and also sewed buttons on the uniforms.

Because we all had to work the few children in camp were not permitted to play. Nevertheless, there were times when we sneaked off to a small tunnel near some pipes and were able to improvise some quiet games.

As in Tomaszow, Rutka worked in the slipper factory, making slippers for German invalid soldiers, while Hanka cleaned clothing in the laundry.

Each workshop had its own SS supervisor, and above them all was a headmaster. The head of the tailor workshop was a German sadist by the name of Eizik.

The SS required a high production quota from each prisoner. Those who fell short got twenty-five lashings on the behind from a guard using a whip with large knots to magnify the pain for the offender, who would receive his punishment while leaning over a trestle. We all had to witness such spectacles, as well as shootings and hangings during Appell, the daily morning and evening prisoner count.

We stood, often in freezing cold weather, as the guards counted us. If the count at Appell did not equal the number of prisoners, we had to remain on our feet, shivering in the cold, our hands and feet frozen, until the count matched. We were so brutalized and terrified that children learned quickly what to do in order to survive, where to hide, how to remain inconspicuous.

Only after morning Appell was completed would we receive a meager breakfast of a slice of black bread and ersatz coffee. In the late afternoon we would get some watery soup, in addition to the bread and ersatz coffee.

"If you knew the person who gave out the soup she gave you from the bottom (which could include pieces of potato or turnip). If you didn't know her, she gave you from the top, so you had water," said Zlacia Warzecha.

Sometimes, though, meals were simply skipped. The deadly combination of minimal nutrition and hard labor caused some Tomaszowers to perish.

"It was always Yom Kippur," remembered Szmul Szampaner. "You were always hungry. There was nothing to eat."

"I said, 'That's it' many times because I was hungry all the time," remembered Genia Rozanski, who witnessed her friend Balcia Reisbaum starve to death. "Who can live without food? In the morning you were up and [you would] find a friend there [dead]; last night you were talking to her."

Blizyn's filthy conditions triggered an outbreak of lice, magnified by the fact that the camp had no bathing facilities for Jewish prisoners. When prisoners had an opportunity they could sneak down to the stream within the camp boundaries to wash their clothes and clean themselves—without soap.

Lack of water in Blizyn was a huge problem, especially since many prisoners also suffered from typhus (a symptom of which is terrible thirst). One of the few reliable and accessible faucets was in the tailor Werkstatt. One day a woman came in with an empty bottle, asking for water. Uncle Jozef was ready to fill it for her when a man from Tomaszow, known to be an informant to the Nazis, told him, "The commandant said you're not supposed to take water out."

"I said, 'Why not give her water? There is typhus here,'" remembered Uncle Jozef. "Since I knew he was a squealer, I said, 'Take off your hand from the bottle. If not, I'll give you [a hit] over the head.' So another man came and said, 'Mr. Tenenbaum, please don't get angry. You go away. I'll bring a bottle of water.'"

Sure enough, the squealer (whose name Uncle Jozef did not recall) told the camp officials. Two days later a guard came into Uncle Jozef's barrack and called out his name along with several others.

"They took us out. They put us to the wall standing with the hands [hands raised] so we thought right away they're going to shoot us, they're going to kill us. Meanwhile there was a lot of commotion in the camp," remembered Uncle Jozef. "We didn't know what's going on, what's going to be. Then they took us to an empty barrack [and] took us off the shoes." The guards confiscated their shoes, a severe punishment because without shoes one could not survive in camp.

When Jozef's wife, Andzia, found out that his shoes had been taken from him, she frantically ran through the camp searching for some footwear to help her husband. Finally, she got hold of a pair of wooden clogs from one of the shoemakers in the workshop and threw them over the fence to Jozef.

"A German saw that and pulled out a board from the fence and he started beating her. She would not cry—very stubborn, my wife. He shouted, 'Why don't you cry?'" said Uncle Jozef. Instead Andzia fainted—the German had broken several of her ribs.

SS abuse of prisoners in Blizyn was so widespread and conditions so oppressive that Tomaszowers who were imprisoned there and later in the infamous Auschwitz death camp said that Blizyn was a far tougher camp, particularly because of the lack of food and sanitation.

Though it was a death camp, Auschwitz was clean. A sign there warned prisoners, "Keep yourself clean because lice is your death," meaning camp officers would kill you if they detected lice on your body. As meager as meals were, at Auschwitz at least they came regularly.

"You got your ration every day, you got your portion, you got a piece of bread, you got a portion of soup," said Josef Zamulewicz.

"That they took you to the crematorium there was nothing you could do about it. But when you were alive at least you got your portion. . . . It was little but it was something," recalled Josef. "Over there in Blizyn there wasn't."

The perspective of having survived Blizyn led Cousin Hanka to recall Auschwitz-Birkenau as almost tolerable.

"Auschwitz was not so bad," said Cousin Hanka. "You had a shower. . . . You had a ration of a piece of margarine, bread, potato soup."

Blizyn's Feared Commander

Blizyn's commander, Untersturmführer Paul Nell was particularly mean and brutal. Nell appeared to be in his early sixties and about five feet eight inches tall. He would walk about camp slowly with his hands behind his back, accompanied by his German shepherd who, upon Nell's command, would instantly attack prisoners.

"This Nell was a beast. He was a very bad Lagerführer. He killed quite a few people," remembered Josef. "There were whippings. Every day you had whippings. . . . Almost every second person got whipped. They said we didn't work enough, we didn't produce enough, every excuse. If you look for an excuse, you find always an excuse to hit somebody," said Josef, who suffered the fate himself.

Nell called his dog "Mensch" (person), while referring to a Jew as a "Hund" (dog). He would command the dog, "Mensch, beis den Hund!" ("Person, bite the dog!"), and in response the German shepherd would chomp into its victim, sometimes ripping off flesh.

"He was a monster," said Genia Rozanski of Nell. "He was so bad. We were afraid to look at him. He sent people to the forest nearby to dig their own graves. Someone did something wrong, they'd be forced to dig a grave and they [Nell's troops] would shoot them. A boy from Bialystok had a spool of cotton he was caught with. Nell sent him to the forest with SS men, and he had to dig a grave. And then he was shot," remembered Genia.

Once, Genia was found taking a piece of white fabric from the workshop. For that she received sixteen whippings.

"I still have marks from this," she said, displaying her scars, more than half a century after the assault.

Still, Genia would sometimes say to her bunkmates, Zlacia and Frymcia Warzecha, "You will see, we will survive."

"You're a *meshugah* [a crazy person]," they responded. And indeed, Genia didn't have confidence in her optimistic prediction.

"They didn't believe it. I didn't believe it. But I said it. I said, 'Let us feel good for a while.' Really, how did we?" asked Genia of her survival.

Nell sometimes toyed with prisoners, once offering a loaf of bread to the person who would jump head first off a bridge that spanned a particularly shallow portion of the creek that ran by Blizyn. Szmul Szampaner, the Z.T.G.S. athlete, took the challenge.

"He said, 'Who's going to dive from that bridge to the water will get a bread,'" remembered Szmul. "I said, 'I'm going to do it.' The water was this deep," said Szmul, measuring five inches. "You jump down, it was about two floors high. I knew I could do it. I trained in Z.T.G.S. So when I dived down, I turned. I went with my feet down. If I went with my head down, I would get killed. I went with my foot down. I was alive. I got a bread. He [Nell] was thinking I'm going to get killed. He was a sadist. He was looking just for dead people. But I knew how to jump."

Jewish security personnel, functioning under German supervision, helped to enforce camp rules. Fishel Samelson suffered a severe beating at the hands of one of them. After working a full night in the tailor shop, he was sent on a work detail to unload newly arrived coal off a train. Weary, Fishel was able to sneak away to his barrack for some sleep. As the work detail was about to return to the barracks, guards counted one man short.

"They came back to the barrack where I was sleeping, and they arrested me and they brought me to the train," said Fishel. "There was SS, four SS guys with their guns drawn. They had those huge dogs with them and then they had a few Jewish policemen. This Jewish policeman, his name was Mintzberg, he was the head of the Jewish police. . . . He jumped on me with his whip. He started to hit me so bad, he knocked my teeth out. I was bleeding all over the place."

It was a vicious assault, but Fishel believed if the Jewish policeman had not attacked him, the SS guards surely would have shot him to death. "When the Germans saw the way I was bleeding . . . they thought, well, he did the job," said Fishel.

Jews picked to lead their barracks sometimes brutalized their fellow prisoners. The *Blockälteste* (head of the barrack in German or *blokowa* in Polish) supervised food distribution, which gave them power and privileges. Overseeing the daily soup rations, a Blockälteste could retain extra soup for herself and sell it for a ring, a watch, or any other valuable. Blockältestes also had living quarters that were partitioned from the rest of the barrack, and at night SS men would sometimes visit their favorite Jewish Blockälteste for sex.

While the barrack supervisors took advantage of their positions of authority, other prisoners went hungry.

"My friend said to me, 'Can you give me a piece of bread? I will give you back,'" recalled Genia. "So my cousin said, 'Where you will buy? Which bakery?'"

"Organizing"

To gain more food some prisoners would "organize," the euphemism we used to describe filching from the camp for the sake of survival. Aunt Eva was among the best.

"I was an organizer," proclaimed Eva. "Let's say they came with a wagon with potatoes. I run, I took a few potatoes, and ate the raw potatoes, was so good. . . . I risk, of course. If the SS man would see, he would kill me."

Eva sewed a gap in her coat, to hide a pot for "organizing" soup.

"When they came with the soup . . . I met them on the way from the kitchen to the barrack. And I was prepared. I had a pot and right away I put in the pot, and I took some soup. And later the people who carried (the soup), I gave them some too. I had a big pot."

Eva's courage was magnified by her conviction that none of us would survive.

"I wasn't afraid at all," added Eva, "because I knew sooner or later we'll go the same way as the people who went to Treblinka."

Eva would sneak items from a camp warehouse, stuffing them under her clothing so they could be traded for food with Poles who came to the camp fence. One of the traders was Eva's husband, Uncle Meylekh. He would throw any valuables that Eva or someone else might have organized, and in turn the Poles at the fence surrounding the camp would throw a salami, bread, or other food in exchange.

"Furious trading would go on for ten minutes, the prisoners throwing their clothes over the fence in exchange for food. 'One jacket,' a prisoner would shout through the wires. 'One loaf of bread,' the answer would come back. And the items would fly in opposite directions over the fence," recalled Cousin Fryda.

It took a lot of bravery to break camp rules in this way. One day a Ukrainian guard in a watchtower saw Meylekh near the wires and shot him in the arm.

"I was standing next to Meylekh Plachta," remembered Fishel Samelson. "The bullet went into one of his arms; it almost ripped his entire arm off. The other bullet went next to my leg, didn't touch me. The bullet just went into the ground."

It was a traumatic event for Uncle Meylekh. A Jewish doctor looked at the arm but could do little since he had no medical implements or supplies. Eventually, though, the bullet came out by itself and his arm healed.

Other people who were caught trading at the wires were beaten in public during the Appell, receiving forty lashes, sometimes more, even those who had bribed the guards.

As bartering took place, prisoners would watch out for each other, using code names for the officers of the camp. "Skurka" was a German who always wore a leather coat. "Kolebaica" was a guard who had a limp and walked like a penguin. "Issac" was a German civilian whose real name was Meyerling and was head of the tailor shop.

The uniforms we had to repair frequently came back from the front splattered with blood and infested with lice. Such an unsanitary working environment, combined with filthy conditions in the barracks, led to the typhus epidemic in camp.

Both my father and I caught the disease at the same time and were sent to the hospital barrack. It was so crowded with ill prisoners that many were lying on the floor. I was on one side of the hospital barrack, among the women, and my father was on the men's side. One day I got up from my bunk bed and walked over to say hello to him. I was very weak, and on my way back I swooned and fell down right in the middle of the barrack floor.

Soon afterwards, a woman who slept near me on the third tier of the hospital bunk received some seltzer from her husband, an especially valuable gift because of the unquenchable thirst that typhus causes. It happened that another woman took the seltzer and drank it. But I was accused of drinking the soda on the assumption that a child would not hesitate to take someone else's property. I was not accustomed to being blamed for something I had not done, so this false accusation made me very upset, and I cried bitterly. Eventually it was discovered that a woman named Rozka Garfinkel had actually drunk the seltzer.

Food was so scarce that I remember once—just once—someone gave me some maize, and I cooked it in the can over the stove that heated the hospital barrack and ate every piece straight from that container. Maize was usually used as chicken feed, but in Blizyn I was glad to get even that.

There were Jewish doctors in the hospital barrack, but they had no medications. Even so, Papa and I recovered, but many people there died of typhus fever.

One day, Untersturmführer Nell called for an Appell to make a selection of children and old people. My father hid Romek and me among a pile of uniforms in the tailor workshop so that the Germans would not find us.

Cousin Fryda recalled being in her barrack when the terror began:

> I heard a truck rumble into the Appell Platz and idle to a halt. A gunshot rang out, then I heard another gunshot and screams.
>
> The next thing I knew, I heard Papa whisper my name: "Fryda! Fryda!" I was surprised to see him, because I knew the SS would punish him if they caught him in my barrack.
>
> "Out quick!" he said. He grabbed my arm and out we ran, dodging from barrack to barrack to avoid being spotted by the guards, and we slipped into his workshop. Shelves piled high with German army uniforms lined the room. Papa pulled out a stack from the bottom shelf and told me to lie down. "Don't move until I come back!" he said. He threw one stack on top of me and piled the rest in front.
>
> From under the uniforms I could hear muffled sounds of gunshots and screams. Hours seemed to pass. I lay there motionless, trying to breathe under the crushing uniforms. Finally I heard Papa whisper my name again: "Fryda." His voice sounded heavy and unnatural.
>
> "I'm still here, Papa," I said, hearing my own muffled voice under the pile of uniforms. Papa pulled the uniforms away and helped me out of my hiding place.
>
> "What happened?" I asked.
>
> "They took the children."
>
> "Where's Dorka?"
>
> "They took her, too."
>
> Papa knelt down and held me close. I could feel his body shake.[2]

Cousin Dorka had been in the camp infirmary, ill with diphtheria. She was among those selected, taken on the truck to a forest near Radom.

"Instead of crying," recalled Fryda, "I imagined Dorka jumping off the truck and hiding in the woods and somebody finding her and taking her in. I kept replaying the scene in my mind with many variations. I never told Mama about my fantasies, but I wondered if she had them too."

If only it were so. Noah Greenspan, a Blizyn prisoner, was ordered onto the truck along with several other men. He witnessed the SS forcing Cousin Dorka and the other children off the truck to face an open pit, then shooting them in the back of their heads. Then the SS ordered Greenspan and the others to bury the bodies. Cousin Dorka was only four years old.

Decades later Cousin Fryda finally learned of the eyewitness account of her sister's murder.

"My fantasies ended and my grieving began. I was finally able to cry for my little sister," said Fryda. "When I was growing up, I had to repress so many tears."

"You had to stay in control. If you were not in control, that was it. If you became hysterical, that was the end. My mother warned me, 'Don't cry. Don't make noise.' I couldn't cry for decades after that. It took many years to thaw out," said Fryda.

In the spring of 1944, a young SS officer by the name of Heller became Blizyn's new Lagerführer, replacing Nell. Heller was tall and walked upright, as opposed to Nell, who was short. More importantly, Heller brought improvements to camp life. He ordered guards to treat prisoners more humanely and permitted those still suffering from typhus time to recover, excusing them from work.

"This guy changed around the whole situation," said Josef Zamulewicz. "You have to say the truth about it. You understand he was a German, everything. But it was no comparison. . . . He was much better than Nell. For example, people organized a piece of bread. By Nell, if you got caught, they killed you right away. By him, he said, 'Oh, let it go.'"

As the Russian army advanced west, the Germans decided to liquidate Blizyn. So, on July 30, 1944, the SS sent us to Auschwitz.

Heller promised us that we would go into Auschwitz without a selection, which is exactly what happened. Rather than parading before Dr. Josef Mengele upon arrival, we went straight to the Birkenau camp of Auschwitz, which most likely saved our lives.

Indeed, after the war, when Heller stood trial in Germany for his part in the Nazi atrocities, several former Blizyn inmates testified on his behalf, which led to a pardon and his release from prison.[3]

5: Auschwitz-Birkenau

A cattle car train with wide-open doors awaited us on the railroad tracks outside camp Blizyn. Rather than sitting at a regular railroad station platform, the train was in the middle of the field just outside camp. The engine huffed and puffed, billowing clouds of smoke, as steam spewed out its sides.

The Germans again loaded us into the cattle cars, squeezing about 120 women into each one. The men, including Tatus and Romek, were in separate cars. There was no room to sit or kneel, so we had to stand during the entire trip; I was tightly sandwiched next to Mama.

"Renia, do you have enough room?" she asked.

"Mama, I'm squeezed, but it's good that we're standing next to the wall. I can get some air from the gaps between the wood slats."

German soldiers sealed shut the cattle car as soon as it was fully packed. Only two tiny windows, one at each end, allowed light into the dark enclosure. Slowly, the train started chugging forward. As we passed stations I could see their names, but the train did not stop at any of them. Instead, it sometimes paused between stations, moved backwards, and then went on again. I did not know our destination.

It was an overnight trip, but to me it seemed like an endless journey. Of course we received no food or water.

Fryda recalled straw on the floor of her car and a pail in a corner.

"People would go there to relieve themselves and then the stuff was hoisted over a high window on the side of the cattle car," she said. "People were crying. People were fainting. It was a miserable, a truly miserable trip."

The train wheels turned slower and slower, then finally stopped. On July 31, 1944, our transport arrived on the platform of Auschwitz II-Birkenau, the massive death camp within the Auschwitz Complex.

"When we came on the station and we saw 'Oswiecim' (the Polish town where Auschwitz is located), we knew we are going to die. We heard about Auschwitz," remembered Genia Rozanski.

SS soldiers unlocked the doors and slid them open. A blinding light greeted us as fierce German shepherds lined the platform.

"ALLE RAUS, SCHNELL HERAUS!" ("All out, quickly, out!"), screamed the soldiers.

The barbarism and ferocity of the Germans knew no bounds. They were like wild animals, screaming and hitting people left and right, seemingly oblivious to blood running down victims' heads, legs, and arms. In fact, it incited them more; they kept shouting and seemed to enjoy their prisoners' suffering and inability to fight back. The Germans were armed with guns and bats, while the Jews were helpless, with no physical strength, no weapons, and no one to back them up. Fortunately, Mama and I were able to run from the train and avoid a beating.

This place seemed eerie as I looked around. A great distance away women standing behind barbed-wire fences were staring at us.

Our transport was one of the few that arrived in Auschwitz without a selection. Evidently because we had arrived from a labor camp, it was taken for granted that the weak, aged, and children had already been eliminated, which was mostly true.

We were ordered to line up in rows of five and were led along the platform and then walkways to a low, long, red-brick building. As we marched toward the building, we saw beautifully manicured hedges framing the path. Inside was a very large room where we were ordered to completely undress and leave our clothing on the benches lining the room. Male prisoners in blue-and-gray-striped prison uniforms walked among us, urging us to surrender to them any gold or diamonds that we possessed because "you will soon go up in smoke."

Some women were picked at random and taken to one side of the room where inmates shaved their entire heads. The self-image of these women was completely deflated with this one act of suddenly having a cleanly shaven bald head.

"I thought we had come to a crazy house," said Frieda Szajewicz. "They cut our hair. We looked like boys. . . . I was by my sister, and she cried, 'Where are you? Where are you?' We were next to each other."

"A Blockälteste spoke Hungarian to us. It was a new language. We thought they were crazy," said Frieda.

"We start looking at each other, we start laughing so much that you can't imagine," remembered Aunt Eva. "This was a tragic laugh. Because it was unbelievable what they could do to the people; some people they looked so awful without the hair. Luckily I remained; me, they didn't cut off the hair," said Eva. Nor did they chop my hair or Mama's.

Spared from a shaving, we were then herded into a huge white room crammed to capacity with the 715 women on our transport, our bodies touching one another. Showerheads hung above. The large door in the rear slammed shut.[1]

It was the first time Fryda had seen naked strangers, which added to the trauma of the event for her. "It was a brutalizing experience on top of all the rest of it," she said.

Suddenly, ice-cold water sprayed down on us.

We emerged dripping wet from the shower to two long tables piled high with dresses. Behind each table were women throwing clothing at each person passing by. If you were short you might get a long dress, and if tall, a short one. I received a gray sackcloth dress and no underwear. Mother's was navy blue, made of rayon. Each of those dresses had previously belonged to women who had arrived at Auschwitz on earlier transports. Rather than shoes we got a pair of terribly uncomfortable wooden clogs. Not everyone, though, was dissatisfied with her new wardrobe.

"I got a beautiful blue dress with polka dots, a silk dress (navy blue with white polka dots)," remembered Aunt Eva. "In the beginning it was good because we arrived in July, but later on . . . a few months later, the weather got bad and I was very cold."

Cousin Fryda was allowed to pick out her dress:

> When the woman in front of me asked for underwear, a curt reply came back, "Be glad you're getting a dress." When it came my turn for clothes, the prisoner who had just spoken looked at me, startled, then at my mother. "I haven't seen a child in so long," she said, her voice much softer now. "Pick out a dress for yourself."
>
> I searched through the pile and found a navy-blue dress with white polka dots. It reminded me of a dress I had worn in happier days. I put it on. It was a summer dress and much too short, but I

wanted it desperately. Mama looked at me and said, "Take something warmer."

"No, I want this dress."

It was no time for argument. "OK. Take it," she said.[2]

Once clothed, we were told to line up in rows, five abreast, and then march past a barbed-wire gate to camp BIIb, one of the many camps located within Birkenau (also known as Auschwitz II). On the right side there were several tables with female prisoners, the *Schreibers* (writers) who transcribed our names, what camp we had come from, and the number to be tattooed onto our left forearms. Our transport was assigned the numbers A-15211 to A-15925.[3] Each woman had to extend her arm, and a female prisoner tattooed the number. Not only were the Nazis tracking us, but they were also trying to dehumanize us as well.

As we stood in line Mama told me, "When they ask how old you are, say sixteen years old."

Sure enough, when I came before the SS supervisor, she posed the question.

"I am sixteen years old. Because of malnutrition I am short and thin," I said. This must have sufficed for the SS woman because I was directed to an inmate who tattooed the number A-15647 on my inner left arm. As she pricked the needle through my skin I kept still and quiet like a grownup so as not to raise suspicion about my true age, which was only eleven.

At that point I ceased being Rena Margulies; I had lost my identity. I became number A-15647, which for the camp personnel was my name. Not only is this number etched into my skin, but it is also etched into my mind till today. I always remember it, even without looking at it. My mother, who was right behind me, was tattooed with the number A-15648.

Frieda Szajewicz also felt the tattoo steal her identity.

"It didn't hurt. It hurt more in the heart. But I felt like a number. I didn't feel like a person, like a dog with a number," said Frieda, who was imprinted with number A-15915.

For Aunt Eva it was more physically painful because the woman who stuck her was particularly aggressive.

"They put in the pen so deep, and it hurt me so much that my number came out crooked because I dragged my hand," remembered Eva, whose permanent reminder was a squiggly "9," the final digit of her A-15669 forearm tattoo.

The 1,614 men in our transport were given the numbers B-1160 to B-2773.[4]

Birkenau's camp BIIb had thirty-four barracks. After getting tattooed we were led to barrack number ten, but we did not stay there long before being transferred to barrack number twenty-two.

The long wooden shelter was lined on both sides with three-storied tiers of bunks. There were no beds, only bare planks of wood, ten women assigned to each one so we were tightly packed like sardines; one person's body fit into the next, just like at Blizyn. If a woman wanted to turn around to change her sleeping position, everybody else on the berth had to do the same. A single blanket was shared among several people.

In the center a brick oven ran lengthwise leading to a chimney. This oven seldom had heat; only upon occasion in winter would there be some warmth emanating from it—but never enough. The guards used it mostly for victimization, forcing prisoners to lean over to receive floggings on the behind.

Any real or imagined infraction was an excuse for punishment: not responding fast enough to orders from the Blockälteste, failing to rise promptly in the morning, slow walking, whispering, sitting or standing in the wrong place at the wrong time, or getting caught with some extra food.

The barrack had no windows, except for small narrow rectangular openings near the ceiling that permitted a minimum of light to enter. The walls were constructed of wood with no insulation. In cold weather we felt the chill from outdoors seeping through the planks, the crevices between them, and the front and back doors.

At the head of the barrack to the right was a partitioned room with a bed, small table, and a chair for the Blockälteste, just as in Blizyn. The Blockälteste was accountable for the barrack's cleanliness, the number of prisoners, and their behavior. She also decided who would get plum jobs, such as fetching and distributing the soup, for which you would receive an extra portion. And, as in Blizyn, by cheating others of their rightful portion, the Blockälteste and her assistant often had additional bread or soup, which they could exchange for valuables that some prisoners had hidden away.

The Blockälteste system was yet another example of how the

Nazis pitted Jew against Jew. Salcia was our Blockälteste, a blond, rather chubby woman of about twenty, who was missing her two front teeth. She claimed to stem from a rabbinical family in Czechoslovakia. The Germans generally chose as heads of the barracks people who were cruel, and Salcia was no exception. She had a nasty disposition. When she got angry her eyes widened with a wild berserk look. She was temperamental and violent, screaming at people in the barrack for every little transgression, actual or not. If we didn't walk fast enough, didn't make the bed neatly enough, or stayed in bed one minute longer than the instant reveille was announced, she hit us with wooden sticks and attacked with a barrage of curses and foul language. She used to scream, "Ja wam dam, ja was naucze!" ("I will give it to you, I will teach you!") and tell us we'd soon be going up in flames. After a day of verbally abusing us, Salcia would unwind through sexual encounters with SS men.

"She slept with German soldiers. Many of the Blockältestes slept with Germans to survive," remembered Frieda Szajewicz.

"This Salcia was such a bastard," recalled Aunt Eva. "She always said that she comes from a rabbi, her grandfather was a rabbi. She was such a nervous wreck. She cursed us, calling us 'Blyzynska kurwa' [whores of Blizyn]. They picked all these bastards for the blockowas. . . . We couldn't stand her, but what could we do? She was appointed from the SS," said Eva.

Salcia woke us in the morning at about four a.m., shouting: "Pobudka wstac, kurwa wasza mac, ja juz krzycze pol godziny a wy spicie kurwy syny pobudka wstac!" ("Get up! Wake up, your mother is a whore! I've been yelling half an hour, and you're still sleeping, sons of bitches. Get up! Wake up!")

Our *sztubowa* or assistant to Salcia was Estusia. She came from Bialystok, was of medium height and build, and had brown hair. Her lover was a Polish worker in the camp. Sometimes when she was cuddled up in her compartment with him, she would ask Nacia Schulmeister from Tomaszow to substitute for her, to ladle out the soup to the prisoners. For that Nacia received either an extra portion of bread or soup, or some honey or margarine on a piece of paper. Many a night Nacia cried into the soup, thinking of how much she wished to give it to her brother Shulim, who was starving in the men's camp.

When we woke there was a mad rush to get to the toilets. Inside of the toilet barrack from one end to the other were rows of gray concrete and stone slabs with alternating holes so that you could approach the toilet seats from either side of the entrance, on the left or right. I could not sit long on the toilet because there was a line of others who needed to go. Then we walked to a long pipe with holes where water trickled out, allowing you to "wash" your hands and catch some water to wet the face. Of course, there was no soap.

Then one had to hurry to straighten out the blanket perfectly flat and smooth because Appell, the prisoner count, began at five thirty promptly. Sometimes it would start earlier, at four o'clock in the morning.

As in Blizyn, we had to stand for hours outdoors in front of the barrack in rows of five until the count was correct. The Blockälteste and other functionaries counted the living persons standing there plus those that had died during the night. If the count did not match they started counting again. Sometimes a person may have been hiding in the barrack, and when the guards found her, they beat her severely, often so brutally that she did not survive the assault.

The counting went on endlessly. We stood there in the summer heat and then in the cold of autumn and winter during damp and rainy days, shivering, our bodies half frozen, for no reason except that the Germans wanted to increase our suffering. When it rained our feet sank into the wet clay soil that felt like a swamp, and once our clogs sank into the earth, it was difficult to extract them. To this day, sixty-nine years later, the tips of my fingers are puffy from the constant exposure to the frigid weather while standing in the Appell.

Meanwhile, Dr. Mengele, the chief camp doctor, walked around the rows of prisoners, whistling arias.

"Food" in Auschwitz

When the Germans were satisfied that the numbers matched and they had tortured us long enough standing on the Appell, four women were sent to the kitchen to fetch warm, dark water that was supposed to be coffee. We also got a small loaf of black bread that we had to share among ourselves. The vat for the coffee was the size of a garbage can, so four women on either side would carry it by holding onto ends of a wooden pole strung through the handles. For their effort they would receive an extra portion. In the evening, when the workers returned from their assigned jobs, we had to stand on Appell again for hours on end till the Germans decided to finish. Once the counting was completed, again four assigned women would head to the kitchen to bring soup.

The soup was a lukewarm, thin liquid, mostly water with some turnips, kohlrabi, cabbage, and rotted potatoes with their skin. If you were lucky and the person serving dipped the ladle deep or if your portion came from the bottom of the barrel, you might get thicker soup with more vegetables in it and, once in a while, a small piece of meat. We each licked the bowl of soup clean, trying to get every drop of available nutrition. That same bowl we used for both eating and urinating at night, as we did in Blizyn, since we were not allowed to leave the barrack after curfew.

The seven people that shared our loaf of bread were all from Tomaszow: Fela Samelson, Dora and Lola Samelson, Genia Drzazga, Aunt Eva, Mama, and me. In our group as we were standing, Aunt Eva was the one who divided the little loaf of black bread among us. She had a good eye and was able to split the loaf equally. Each one of us carefully watched the division to ensure the portions were equal, though we never argued about our shares. Some time later Aunt Eva made the process a bit more exact, fashioning a little balance scale out of a stick and some cotton thread in order to weigh an equal portion for everyone, about one and a half inches by two inches for each of us.

"When we got the bread I had a good eye," remembered Aunt Eva.

"In order nobody should think one got a tiny millimeter bigger than the other, I put one of the girls, and I stand in back of her, and I said, 'For whom is this portion? For whom is this portion?' So no one would say, 'You gave this one a bigger, this one a smaller,'" remembered Eva. "We cared for each other because everyone was in the same situation."

Not every group of friends was so disciplined. With food in short supply there were disagreements and deception. Some prisoners would sell an item of value, such as cigarettes, for the promise of an extra piece of bread, which often would never materialize.

Other inmates resorted to stealing food from their fellow prisoners; there were even organized muggings in the men's camp.

"When you walked on the street a little next to the barrack, you could suddenly be surrounded by a bunch of Russian prisoners, and one grabbed your bread and ran away," recalled Fishel Samelson. "And the rest wouldn't let you out to run after. I saw it happen to some people."

Fishel was lucky enough to gain employment that provided a steady supply of nourishment, cleaning clothing for a Nazi officer. Then he landed an even better job, thanks to his tailoring skills, which provided a surfeit of food.

> I was standing in an Appell one evening, an SS officer calls my number. I said, "My God, finally I got a place where maybe I could survive." I had two, three friends, Tomaszowers who worked for the SS tailoring shop. And they needed another tailor so they gave the SS man my number. That's how I got into the SS tailoring shop, and I worked there for three months under the best conditions you could ever think of in a concentration camp: used to get all kinds of food, warm all day long, working my tailoring, and I was able to get at least a loaf of bread or more on my way home. And that's how I used to help my sisters. I used to give them every night a piece of bread. I used to give them little cigarettes that they can . . . [bribe] someone there to give them a little food. Every night, like religiously, I used to throw a bread over the fence on the other side.
>
> Every morning at six a.m. in the morning I had a whole line of Tomaszowers next to my place where I was sleeping for food, because the food that was handed out in the barrack I didn't eat. I didn't need it so I used to give it to these men. One, two, three, four, I recall very vividly.
>
> The head of the SS kitchen was not a youngster, he was an older guy but he had all kinds of girlfriends, you know, Polish girlfriends [who lived outside of the camp]. When you go to see a girlfriend in the evening, you don't have any place where to buy a box of candy or flowers or whatever. So he used to come in with a piece of cloth into the shop, and he'd say, 'Felix' or to my partner, 'Can you make me a skirt? I have a date tonight.' Of course we'd make a skirt for him. And all he'd do is give me a piece of paper, and in the morning I went into the SS kitchen and I used to get, without exaggeration, a container of food, rice and milk with sugar, you've never seen anything like this. I didn't need it, and I had a

> friend, Biederman, he used to help me shlep it from this place. And there was a group of girls, they used to work in the crematoria, and I used to go there and hand it out each one a quart of rice soup.

Szmul Szampaner found extra food working for the Lagerkommando. After trains arrived and unloaded their prisoners, the Lagerkommando would clean up the cattle cars. That provided an opportunity for Szmul to find food, often in the hands or garments of prisoners who had died en route or on the floor since arriving prisoners dropped food as they were forcibly evacuated from the cars.

"I had a lot to eat there," said Szmul, who quickly acclimated to the grim task of carrying out dead bodies.

Such a steady supply allowed Szmul to give provisions and tobacco for bribes to his brother Leibish when they met in Birkenau, just before Leibish was sent on a transport to a Dachau subcamp.

"He said, 'Keep this tobacco. It will help you out,'" recalled Leibish.

More typically, prisoners stole—"organized"—from the camp itself: potatoes, vegetables, bread, anything edible that could be smuggled.

As in Blizyn, Eva got hold of a pot and used her sewing skills to maximize her chances of swiftly stealing from the soup container by creating two deep pockets, each large enough to conceal the pot.

When the soup carriers came out of the kitchen, Eva was prepared. She would swoop in on the barrel as it was being transported, quickly dipping in her pot, then running off with her prize.

"I risk a lot. I risk a lot because I thought to myself, 'Anyway I'm going to the gas chamber, sooner or later.' So I don't have to think too much of it," she said.

One day guards caught Eva. They punished her immediately, forcing her to kneel the rest of the day on sharp pointed pebbles at the front of the camp while holding a heavy stone above her head. At the end of the day, when Eva returned to the barrack, she said it was as if she had lost her hands, they were completely numb after hurting terribly for hour after hour, and her knees and legs were covered with blood, pierced by the sharp pebbles.

October 12 was Eva's birthday. It was a cloudy, drizzly day with no one outdoors. It so happened that I was walking near the kitchen barrack, located at the front of the camp. A truck had just delivered a load of cabbages and pulled away. One large cabbage rolled right in front of my feet. I looked around. To the left. To the right. No one was near. So I picked up this large cabbage, so big that I—a little girl—couldn't fully wrap my arms around it. Quickly I darted in back of the buildings so that no one would notice me, sneaked into our barrack through the back door, then gave the cabbage to my aunt as a birthday gift. I don't think that she could have ever gotten a better present since food was more precious than possessions. We shared and ate the raw cabbage for the next several days.

Food was an obsession. My big joy was to tell my mother and aunt what I would eat after the war. Before we went to sleep each night, as we lay on the planks I made up a menu consisting of my favorite foods, including twenty frankfurters, fifteen sprats, ten loaves of bread, five dozen eggs, and a dozen blueberry turnovers for breakfast. The larger the quantity of food the more satisfied I seemed.

One day I heard a rumor that a Blockälteste in one of the barracks near the front gate of the camp had an extra supply of milk. She was inviting children (there were only a handful of us in the camp) to have a cupful of milk. I ran after the other kids, joined by cousin Fryda, who was in another barrack. When we arrived several women prisoners sat us down on four benches surrounding a table on which they placed large loaves of thickly sliced white bread generously spread with butter. Each child was given a slice of bread and a cup of milk. I was grateful for this cup of milk, and I drank it thinking, "This is the last cup of milk that I'll have for a very long time. This is my last opportunity, so I should drink it to the very last drop and be grateful for it." Before the war I had always been a fussy eater; milk in particular was not one of my favorite beverages. But this time I eagerly drank the milk with gusto. I was sorry that my mother could not share in this feast, and I am certain Fryda felt the same about her mother.

In the following days and weeks I approached that barrack to check for the chance of another feast, but sure enough, it was a one-time event. We starved each day, only dreaming of full, regular meals.

"I said, 'Maybe some day we will eat so that we will never be hungry any more,'" remembered Genia Rozanski. "I said if I will be free, I will sit the whole day and the whole night and eat."

Auschwitz: Death in the Air

Mama made it her chief task to ensure that I stayed alive. So she tried to protect me, keeping me with her in the back row during roll call, surrounded on all sides by adults to minimize the chance I might be chosen for work squads. During the day we stayed near the barrack with a few other people who had not been picked for a work detail.

When I caught measles as an epidemic spread through the camp, she made sure I covered my face to hide the red spots; otherwise I could have been taken and killed. I must have had a very mild case because it was relatively inconspicuous and went away in a short time.

We had no doubt about the function of Auschwitz. Prisoners were marched away, never to be seen again. Fire would rise from the crematoria every night. The stench of burning flesh permeated the air. Everyone knew, even the children like me.

"The fear in Auschwitz. We thought every day we'd go to the crematoria," said Frieda Szajewicz. "Nine times we went before [Dr. Josef] Mengele," who would often send prisoners to their death. At night [before curfew] I went to the toilet. I could see the fire over all of Auschwitz. And I thought, 'I'll go there. This will be my death.'"

Szmul Szampaner watched the smoke blowing from the crematoria, and in his mind he saw body parts emerging.

"I saw every day the chimney. We saw the chimney and nighttime, wintertime especially, you look at the chimney, you see a hand, feet flying out from the chimney. Day and night was burning."

Many a day, I stood at the camp wires, looking out toward the railroad tracks that regularly delivered trains pulling carloads of people. They arrived from many countries, from all over Europe—Belgium, France, Holland, Hungary, Italy, Rhodes, Slovakia, Czechoslovakia, and of course, Poland, some dressed in beautiful clothing, women in hats, wearing high-heeled shoes, carrying expensive luggage, evidently taken by complete surprise upon arrival. Entire families with children. These people seemed to know nothing of the inferno that burned here.

I saw from a distance how they were rushed, separated and then presented before the SS for a selection. At other times the complete transport was herded immediately to the crematoria, and all you saw were the constant flames of fire shooting straight into the sky through the tall chimneys that looked like factory smokestacks.

When I looked at those fires bellowing from those smokestacks, I made myself a plan: When the Germans send us to the crematoria I will tell the people with me in line that this is a crematorium and that we should put up resistance and not be taken to be burned. The sign by which I would recognize the crematorium would be the wires sticking out of the tall chimneys. I realize now that a plan like that would have been futile because the Germans were armed and ready to shoot at a moment's notice. But this was my fantasy and helped to keep up my morale under trying circumstances.

Auschwitz Slave Labor

Since Auschwitz was a death camp, not a labor camp, few of the surviving tailors from Tomaszow had work practicing their needle trades. Those who had regular jobs contributed to the functioning of the camp or repaired facilities.

Sometimes several men came to work in the women's camp. Whether they were there to fix the showers, the toilet barracks, or do some other job, I don't know. Once, I heard one of them sing a song to one of the female prisoners: "Jeszcze biegne wzdluz wagonu, az pociag mknie, do widzenia nie zapomne cie, i bede tesknil, za twa miloscia za twym spojrzeniem" ("I am still running along the length of the wagon as the train rushes. Farewell. I shall never forget you. And I will yearn for your love, for your glance").

Many prisoners assigned jobs were simply put to work for work's sake, to further torture and drain them. Frieda Szajewicz suffered such a fate one morning at three a.m. when guards woke her and ordered her to work in the snow moving buckets of water from one pond to another. Totally exhausted, she made a desperate prayer. "I asked [God] to be taken to the crematoria. I am finishing with life," said Frieda. Aunt Eva labored at the Vistula River, carrying heavy stones from one pile to another, supposedly to regulate the river flow. When she returned late in the day, her dress was wet from trudging through the river. She would place it under her body each night to let it dry before putting it back on in the morning. Sleeping on the wet dress nightly left her with rheumatism, from which she suffered for the rest of her life.

Camp guards magnified her torture one day by taking her and

other female prisoners to the showers. After pouring cold water on them, the women were left to stand naked and wet, shivering for hours. Finally they started screaming and yelling for their clothes. In response, the Germans sprayed more cold water on the naked women. Some of them got sick and died from hypothermia.

One German guard, at least, showed compassion for Eva while she worked at the Vistula. He pointed to her and indicated that he had left a sandwich not far from where she was working. Every day she went to this spot and found a sandwich, which helped her survive.

Later on in Birkenau Eva worked in the so-called weaving squad, which ripped rags into strips and then tied them together, for the purpose of cleaning gun barrels, extremely difficult because tearing the dirty rags resulted in dust so unbearable that one could hardly breathe.

Of all the labor assignments in Auschwitz-Birkenau, the most ghastly was that of the Sonderkommando, the prisoners who worked in the crematoria by huge ovens, burning the corpses of people who had just been gassed to death. Wolf Kaiser once had a close-up look, when SS guards assigned him and several others to use a wheelbarrow to transport three corpses there.

> The crematoria looked rather like an old fashioned oven in a European bakery, with the difference that instead of baking bread, they baked Jewish bodies.
>
> The dead bodies were brought in from the gas chambers to the crematoria, and dumped on the floor in front of the oven. The oven was about six steps down the floor level. On the floor dead bodies of men and women were scattered about. Only strong Jewish men were picked from among the inmates to work at and around the crematoria. After a time working there they too were killed, and others were picked to replace them.
>
> At the oven where Wolf and the others dumped the bodies picked up from the ramp was a Jewish man working the oven. He was feeding the ovens with the Jewish bodies. While Wolf was on the floor, the man six steps lower looked a little heavy and chubby. (The Germans fed them well.) The man had difficulty lifting the whole bodies to shove them into the oven. To make it easier for himself, with an axe he chopped the bodies into parts and threw

> them piecemeal into the oven.
>
> The poor fellow had scary eyes, with a sad face which said, "You might still have a chance, but I, I am condemned for sure."
>
> Talking to the man was strictly *verboten* (forbidden); besides, there was no time, being rushed back to the camp. They looked at each other with sad eyes without saying a word. But the man shoved a full loaf of bead at Wolf, saying, "Hide it, you must be hungry."[5]

Essential for those who had to work in Auschwitz was a decent pair of shoes, critical for surviving snow in the winter and constant mud all other seasons. "When you didn't have shoes, you were dead," declared Szmul Szampaner. Szmul was able to find a good pair of shoes by taking them from the feet of a corpse lying in a train car he was cleaning. "That's how it was. This is life. Took off the shoes on him and I put on," said Szmul. "I was wearing the shoes for years. I couldn't take off. Why? When I take them off, they steal. They steal the shoes."

Aunt Eva got a good pair from her Blockälteste. "Once I came back to the barrack, we walked maybe two, three miles one way, the mud was so bad my shoes fell apart. . . . I came back to the barrack. So the blockowa said to me, 'Go and bring the soup.' So I said, 'How could I go? I have no shoes. Give me a pair of shoes, I go.' She had plenty. She went in her room, and she brought me a pair of wonderful—those shoes saved my life. She gave me the shoes, and I went for the soup. And then I passed by the gate and saw that the blockowas they had good underwear. I saw a pair of . . . the underwear. *Nu,* so I grabbed it. It was wool, and I was safe to go on the Auserkommando" (Eva's slave labor work detail outside of camp).

But protecting your feet offered no security from SS punishment. One day while working in the Vistula River, Aunt Eva washed her face. An SS guard saw and ordered her to kneel all day until the Kommando returned to the barrack.

Auschwitz: Romek's Fate

Papa and my brother Romek were together in barrack number 10 within Camp BIIa, the division of Birkenau housing all men from our transport, located adjacent to our camp BIIb. Mother and I could meet Papa and Romek behind our barracks, where we were separated by two rows of electrified barbed wire. It was a great comfort to see each other and to be able to exchange a few words.

A transport of children that had arrived from the Kovno ghetto was also housed in my brother's barrack. The Jewish New Year was nearing. On Jewish holidays the Germans always made our lives even more painful than they already were, enforcing all kinds of severe torture on those days, as if our constant persecution, starvation, imprisonment, and enslavement were not enough.

Cousin Rutka, who had lived with us in Tomaszow, was also in Birkenau. One day she stood at the wires looking at Romek and Papa. Romek was sick with measles at the time, weakened from the diet and the emotional strain of incarceration. He was wearing a white shirt from the *Revier*—the area of the camp that included the hospital barrack. Rutka said to Romek, "Zobaczyc, Romek, juz wyzdrowiec wkrotce," ("You will see, Romek, you will recover soon"). Romek must have been very dejected because he answered Rutka, "Ja juz nigdy nie wyzdrowieję" ("I will never recover").

On the fateful first day of Rosh Hashanah, September 18, 1944, the German doctor Heinz Thilo made a selection. The children had to line up five in a row and stand between barracks number 9 and number 10. Dr. Thilo was dressed in his SS uniform, wearing white gloves. He walked in front of the children, looking carefully at each child. Near him walked a prisoner, a Schreiber. After a while he took off the glove from his right hand. With this uncovered hand he called over selected boys with his finger saying, "Komm." The Schreiber wrote down the numbers of the children.[6]

After the selection Mother came to the wires where Tatus and Romek were standing. With tears in his eyes, Romek threw the piece of bread he had received that morning over the wires and said, "Mama, take it."

"Why are you giving me your bread?" Mama asked. "Did they put you on the list?"

"No," Romek replied and started crying. "Mama, you take it. I won't need it anymore," he said, then ran back into the barrack.

Romek had so much courage that he did not tell Mama he was on the list.

Later a truck came, the boys walked out from the barracks in white shirts, and they loaded my brother Romek together with the other children recorded on the list, including sixty-five boys from

Kovno. The truck left in the direction of the crematorium. That's how my brother was killed on the first day of Rosh Hashanah, September 18, 1944. He was nine years old. He did not do anyone any harm. His only crime was that he was a Jew.

Mother just could not take the death of Romek. She became very depressed, could not eat, and when she did attempt to do so, she would vomit it all.

Eva knew that Mama suffered deeply from the loss of Romek, so she made up a story to comfort her, claiming that at the front of the camp gate she heard that the children taken on the truck were in an adjoining camp and that Romek was among them. I don't know if Mama had any hope that Eva's story might be truthful because she never told me.

Papa was heartbroken. The next month he was sent on a transport out of Auschwitz-Birkenau.

Auschwitz: Uprising

One day, standing outside the barrack, I heard an explosion, which was followed by the sight of a fire in the distance. Perhaps it was a military battle, I thought, an indication the front was nearing. But I did not know. Not until after the war did I learn it was an attack on Crematorium IV, which burst into flames on October 7, 1944.

Three Jewish women employed in the Weichsel-Union Metallwerke, Ala Gertner, Ester Wajsblum, and Regina Sapirstein, stole explosives from the plant's depot. They gave the explosives to Roza Robota, a Polish Jew working in the personal effects camp bordering the Crematorium IV compound, who passed the stolen material to a Jewish prisoner named Wrobel, a worker in the Sonderkommando. On October 7, 1944, members of the Sonderkommando staged an uprising during which they blew up and set Crematorium IV on fire, in the process killing several German soldiers. Most of the men escaped but were later captured and killed. Ala Gertner, Roza Robota, Regina Saperstein, and Esther Wajsblum were captured, tortured, and hanged publicly before other inmates on January 5, 1945. At the time of her hanging, Roza Robota called for vengeance.

Though they endured abusive conditions under strict surveillance, these prisoners through a concerted effort were still able to destroy a crematorium, an act of supreme heroism, one that may have saved my life.

Auschwitz: FKL

In October the SS conducted a selection among a large group of women. We were lined up, walked out of camp BIIb along the road that traversed camps BIId and BIIe and then into FKL, Frauen Konzentrationslager (women's concentration camp), a complex of barracks within Birkenau, located on the far side of the railroad tracks.

Cousin Fryda recalled our mothers' show of resistance.

> The Kapos came into our barrack and told us to follow them. A few minutes later we arrived at a building with a sign over the door that said Badeanstalt (bathhouse). An SS guard told us to line up. I stood in line with Mama. Renia and her mother were right behind me, the rest of my aunts ahead of us. A few minutes later an SS officer in a black uniform arrived, impeccably dressed with a gold rosette in his lapel, white gloves, his boots smartly polished. The SS guard addressed him as Hauptsturmführer (captain), and I overheard someone mutter, "Mengele." Mama squeezed my hand.
>
> Dr. Josef Mengele turned and faced us from the head of the line. He began motioning people to the left and to the right. Each passed through one at a time. I noticed that the younger women were going to the right and the older women and children to the left. When Mama and I came to the front of the line, he motioned me to the left. Mama refused to let go of my hand.
>
> "No, you go to the right," Mengele said, but Mama held fast.
>
> The SS guard stepped forward and tried to pull us apart.
>
> "No, no!" Mama called out. "I want to go with her."
>
> "You heard the Hauptsturmführer," the guard said. "Go to the right!"
>
> Mama still refused to let go. When the guard saw we were holding things up, he slammed his truncheon on her shoulder and said, "Then go with her!"
>
> Renia was next in line. Her mother refused to let go, too. The SS guard apparently not wanting to hold up the line again, motioned them to the left, saying, "Okay, go with them."[7]

We were sent toward the showers, where we undressed. Several women had menstrual blood running down their inner thighs. We stood there naked for a long time in front of a big black door, which people said was the door to the gas chamber. While we waited stark naked, freezing, some of the women complained. At that point the Germans poured ice-cold water on us to magnify our suffering. The door never opened, though. That day our lives were saved, probably a result of the prisoner uprising that had destroyed Crematorium IV, forcing the Germans to discontinue use of the gas chamber on the opposite side of the door.

Guards then led us to the barracks, block number 25 in the Frauen Konzentrations Lager, which was supposed to be a holding block for the gas chambers. We stood there naked and shivering all day. Finally, near the end of the day, some damp clothing was thrown into the room, and each one of us took a garment to cover ourselves. As a punishment for requesting clothing, we did not receive our evening meal.

One day an SS woman saw me and Cousin Fryda, ten months my junior, and asked my mother whether she would like to save us.

"Of course," Mama replied.

"Then let me take them where they will be safe."

That's how Fryda and I ended up in the twins' barrack, where Dr. Mengele was performing his experiments on twins. Every day children were taken out from the barrack, many never to return; others came back with bandages, visibly weaker and withdrawn.

One set of twins from Belgium, a thin girl with nice black hair and her brother, were given white bread and milk, a luxury. The girl, who was coughing, drank some of the milk and gave the rest to Fryda. Knowing that tuberculosis, or consumption, is highly contagious and can be transmitted through mouth contact with contaminated milk, I led Fryda to the toilet, so as not to embarrass the girl, and insisted that she spill the milk into the toilet bowl rather than drink it and get sick.

About four dozen children were housed in the barrack. Fryda and I shared a thin pad of straw on the third tier of a bunk. Our only covering was a blanket so worn out you could see through it. Fryda remembered us cuddling for warmth the first night, then being separated. The women who were supervising the bunk said, "You cannot snuggle and you must take your clothes off. You have to be separate." We had to take our clothes off and freeze under these transparent blankets. The children on the lower bunks got better blankets—we were on the third level because we were slightly older than them—and I was very jealous because we were so cold.

As soon as we woke early in the morning we dressed quickly and made our beds. We shared the task so that every day a different person made the beds for the entire berth. One day it was my turn. I jumped down from the top tier, but upon landing my anklebone suddenly dislodged from its socket. I was in agony. With all my might I tried to push the bone into its proper position, fearing that if I were not in top shape I might be selected to go to the crematorium. Finally after several tries my ankle bone snapped back into alignment to my great relief. The other children were very sympathetic and gladly volunteered to make the bed, an example of the cooperation among us.

The women working in the barrack tried to keep us amused, playing "ring around the rosie" and circle games, which was extremely strange, given the fact that we were prisoners in a death camp, surrounded by the stench of daily mass murder.

"What's going on here? This is so crazy," thought Fryda. "Why would we be playing when this is going on around us and we're going to all die anyway? And the songs were sung in German," which further added to the bizarre aspect of the artificial play.

As the other children participated, I sat alone. Separation from my mother was extremely hard, and without her I became very depressed. She was the only person upon whom I depended completely. Several days after I entered the barrack, some mothers came to the back door to see their children for just a short time. Aunt Eva arrived with a little note written in my mother's distinctive handwriting on a small scrap of paper. Mama wrote that she did not have any shoes and was working in the hospital. Eva explained that my mother's shoes had been stolen and therefore she could not come to see me. But I refused to believe the note was from my mother, even though the handwriting was hers. Since the rule in Auschwitz was if you did not see a person they were surely dead, I assumed my mother had died and began mourning for her.

In fact, Mama did have a job in the hospital barrack at camp BIIe. A dentist from Tomaszow, Dr. Maniusia Hanel, who had passed as a gentile through the war and was now working in the Birkenau hospital in a position of authority, had arranged for Mama and Aunt Andzia to be transferred to the hospital.

Andzia told Fryda to feign severe pain on her right side, as if she were suffering a gallbladder attack. Fryda did as her mother said, and soon afterwards she was sent to the hospital barrack.

With each passing day I was getting weaker. The cold, lack of food, and mourning were all taking their toll. I fell ill and finally was also transferred to the hospital barrack. But when I arrived Mama was not there. Aunt Andzia was caring for Fryda, combing her hair with her fingers.

"Your mother was sent out of the camp a few minutes ago," said Andzia. "Go over to Maniusia and see if she can get your mother back."

It took me not more than a second to run over to Maniusia.

"Dr. Hanel, please return my mother back to me! I was transferred from the children's barrack. I need my mother! I cannot live without her. Please!"

It was a plea from my heart, which must have deeply touched Maniusia because she quickly directed me.

"Go to the shower barrack, find your mother, and bring her back here."

The shower barrack was filled with women, hundreds, who were standing under showerheads, cleansing themselves before leaving Auschwitz on a transport. But I was able to find my mother.

"Mama, Maniusia says that you can go back with me to the hospital barrack!" I exclaimed.

"Renia! I'm so happy to see you, to have you here with me," Mama responded with a big smile as water poured from above.

She dressed in her navy-blue dress in a jiffy, and we returned to the hospital barrack.

Though we were reunited, the separation from Mama had left its mark. I had been so convinced she had been killed that it took me a while to adjust to the reality that indeed I had found my mother and she truly was alive.

Auschwitz: Coping

People had different ways of coping with imprisonment and the constant threat of death surrounding us. Some turned to music. Zlacia would whistle sometimes. Frieda Szajewicz would sing, as would Aunt Eva, who said it helped ease her pain. Among her favorite songs was a Polish tune called, "Santa Felicia."

"It gave you a little life because if you sing, you forget all the problems. Not all, but it gave you a little lift," said Eva. "Sometimes I said to my friend, 'We will survive. We will survive, and we will walk someday on the boulevards of Paris.'"

Others relied upon prayer. But witnessing the nightmare of mass murder challenged many prisoners' belief in God. How could there be a God that would permit man to perpetrate such atrocities on his fellow man? To build and operate factories of death?

Try to imagine how baffling and overpowering such questions were to eyewitnesses, especially people who had been religiously observant. Such issues loom large today and will for eternity. Our faith is further challenged with each act of genocide that has occurred since the Holocaust.

Personally, I never prayed while in camp; I didn't even think of it. But even in the face of such horrors some retained their faith. To whom else could they turn? And so, in their hearts, the pious still prayed, especially for divine intervention that might end their nightmare. To pray openly, though, placed one at danger. Those who did, especially on Jewish holidays, were sent away to the crematoria.

Some held on to their beliefs in other ways. Genia Rozanski recalled fasting on Yom Kippur, an act of faith that forcibly lasted into the following day since she did not receive any soup or bread upon the conclusion of Yom Kippur. Why did she fast, I asked?

"Because it was a Jewish holiday. I said maybe this will help me."

"Do you think it helped you?"

"Maybe. I believe in God."

"Did you always believe?"

"Sometimes I hesitated."

"We were waiting for a miracle," said Frieda Szajewicz. "We were always thinking there will be a miracle. Even in Auschwitz we thought maybe there will be something. We had hope. Maybe, maybe. But, at the same time, every day I thought I'd die."

Tomaszowers in Other Camps

As the Allies advanced, the front edged toward Auschwitz, leading the SS to transfer some prisoners to other camps.

Aunt Eva left on the last transport from Auschwitz to the Bergen-Belsen concentration camp on December 31, 1944, along with Cousin Hanka Lew (who had lived with us in Tomaszow and cared for me), and five other Tomazowers, Mania Warzecha, Fela Samelson, Rose Szyk, Mania Markowicz, and Sala Kenigsztejn. All were given some food for the trip to Bergen-Belsen, a loaf of bread, thick jam called *lekvar*, and a big slice of salami.

While not a death factory like Birkenau, Bergen-Belsen presented its own dangers. Anyone who fell ill was simply tossed out into the cold and left to die, recalled Sala. "The people were lying in snow, they were dying. It was terrible, the screaming, the crying, terrible, terrible."

Other women from Tomaszow went to an ammunition factory in Whilisthal, including Cousin Rutka Lew, Genia Rozanski, Zlacia Warzecha, and her sister Frymcia Warzecha. While they worked as slaves, they did live together in a house where they enjoyed much-improved accommodations, in spite of abuse from a harsh Lagerführer, a tall blond woman named Helena Klaupfig.

"New Year's one woman got a piece of cake, [and she] brought some of the cake" into the barrack, Genia Rozanski recalled. "The Lagerführer did a search." Klaupfig found the cake and confronted Genia.

"If you tell me who brought this cake, I won't cut your hair," she warned. When Genia refused, Klaupfig violently chopped Genia's hair, extracting chunks of skin in the process.

Some of Tomaszow's men endured a different path of suffering, shuttling from one concentration camp to another.

Direct from Blizyn about 100 prisoners, including Uncle Jozef, Nuta Romer, Srulek Markowicz, and Chaim Modrzewski, were sent to Plaszow concentration camp in the southern portion of Krakow. (Plaszow was adjacent to industrialist Oskar Schindler's enamelware factory, where he employed and tried to protect about 900 people from abuse in the camp.)

In Plaszow they were put to work making saddles for two weeks. The saddle shop provided an opportunity to use their tailoring skills to sew clothing that they could then trade for food.

"We had to help ourselves as much as possible. Since I was a tailor I was sewing some jacket or pair of pants," Uncle Jozef said. "This was thrown over the fence to the Poles. . . . They had food so we threw over there a piece of clothing, and they threw over a loaf of bread, two loaves of bread. Mr. Markowicz was the merchant. I was doing the work [tailoring] and Mr. Romer was doing the work."

From Plaszow Uncle Jozef and the others went to Wieliczka, Poland, to work in salt mines, then in September 1944, to Melk, Austria, a subcamp of the slave-labor camp Mauthausen. There, in Austria's Tyrol Mountains, they were part of a construction crew building secret hangars to protect German aircraft that were vulnerable sitting on airfields.

To protect themselves against the cold, they would place empty cement mix bags under their striped prisoner uniforms, which was forbidden.

"One day [I] came back from work, I was wearing a paper bag. They caught me and gave me twenty-five lashings," remembered Uncle Jozef.

Conditions were brutal. If a prisoner died or was killed while working, the others had to carry him back to camp on a stretcher so the evening Appel—which sometimes lasted for hours—would match the morning count.

To survive, Uncle Jozef again used his ingenuity and tailoring skills.

> I was dreaming if I could get into the [tailor] shop I would survive, I would be saved. Many times I went into the shop there and talked to the foreman. He was a German, he was a [convicted] criminal. [Shirts for criminals were emblazoned with green arrows.] I went in to talk to the Kappo, and I said to him, "I'm a good tailor, take me in to work." So he said, "I cannot take you in. You're a Jew. You're not allowed to do it. That's what the order is."
>
> But later on, a few days later, I found out that they made a suit for the commandant and they ruined the suit. So this man, the shoemaker said, "Now is the moment you go in, and he will take you in." When I was standing in roll call I was measuring up the commandant, and I was dreaming if I could make him a suit I would be saved.
>
> So I go into this Kappo, and I tell him, "I heard you made a suit for the commandant and it didn't come out good. I will fix it for you."
>
> He said, "You will fix it for me? You're sure you will fix it for me? If you're not going to fix it right, you're going to be shot."
>
> I said, "I'm sure I'm going to fix it. It will be right."

So he was not a tailor, but here he saw how sure I am, so he said, "Go over to the table, and draw a suit. I want to see how you do it." Naturally it was easy for me, and he saw I know what I'm doing. And he said, "OK. Come in tomorrow to work in the shop."

So I said, "I cannot come in. Kappo, you got to go to the office where they make out the list of the numbers who go out to work, because if you want me to come in they have to replace me with another person. Otherwise it's going to be a whole terrible thing." So he went over with me there and said he is taking this tailor and you should replace [him with] another person. Going back, he said to me, "Come into the shop." It was eleven o'clock at night already. And Mr. [Nuta] Romer and Mr. [Srulek] Markowicz were standing outside anxious—the results, what's going to be?

And I came back to the shop, and he says, "You are hungry?" And I said, "Yes, sure, I'm hungry." So he gave me half a loaf of bread and marmalade and some salami.

Uncle Jozef laughed at this point, then cried as he retold the story.

I was laughing. These people [his friends], they didn't believe their eyes that I got these things. The next day I went in to work there, and he brought me the suit. He showed me the suit. I put it on myself.

When I looked at him [the commandant], when I was standing there on the roll call I measured him. He had just the same figure as I, same height, same everything. And also since I'm a good tailor, I knew this is a uniform. A uniform has to be fitted. The armholes have to be very high; he should be able to raise his arms.

Uncle Jozef said, lifting his arms as if to salute.

If it's good here, everything goes up, the whole thing goes up. So I put on the jacket and uniform myself, and right away I saw what's wrong. So I had to rip it apart. I had to take out the collars, the sleeves, the shoulders and cut it down so much, and I fixed the suit. I fixed the suit, and it was in the evening. He brought it over to the commandant, and he tried it on and he said, "It's good now."

He wanted me to do him a favor. He disregards that I'm Jewish. . . . And he said, "Now I want you to make for him a new

> suit, suits, a coat, whatever, for the wife." So I said to the Kappo, "I cannot do it by myself, I mean with these tailors. I need my own tailors which they know [how to do a good job]." So he said, "Who are they" So I brought in these three tailors, Mr. Markowicz, Mr. Romer, and Mr. Modrzewski. I took them in and [in] the worst time we were sitting there and working in that shop.
>
> Meanwhile, the cooks found out there is a good tailor. You know they were not hungry. The cooks they had food, women, everything that they wanted. So, they came in and said to me that I should make for them suits. I should fix them the suits. So I said, "If you give me food, a kettle of soup, bread, I'll make it for you." So every day Nuta Romer and Srulek Markowicz went over, they got a kettle of food, and I was helping already these paisanos, these landsleit from my town.[8]

And so Uncle Jozef, Nuta Romer, and Srulek Markowicz worked in Melk in relatively comfortable circumstances until February of 1945, when American bombings forced an evacuation for two weeks to another Mauthausen subcamp in Ebensee, Austria.

Liberation from Auschwitz-Birkenau

In early January 1945 Mama, worried about my fading strength, asked a doctor in the hospital barrack to examine me. After the exam he said, "Your daughter has tuberculosis. If the war does not end within three weeks, I doubt she can survive."

Mama herself was weak as well, particularly after suffering a severe fall on the ice while carrying a large garbage can filled with feces to the latrine. She tumbled hard to the ground, badly bruising herself as the excrement spilled around her.

The Russian army was advancing toward Auschwitz-Birkenau, leading the Germans to announce a plan to evacuate the Birkenau camp and burn it down. An order came to queue up for a march out of Birkenau, as trains were no longer departing with prisoner transports. We joined a huge line with hundreds of other prisoners near Birkenau's exit. Giant searchlights at the gate illuminated flakes of snow falling in the evening as the line inched forward. We waited and waited, but there were still many people ahead of us. By the time we approached the exit it was very late. The guards closed the gate and announced, "You will burn together with the camp." Wearily, I trudged back to the barrack and lay down, exhausted, to an uneasy sleep. The next morning we again dragged ourselves to the gate, trying to leave the camp along with the other stragglers. Standing in line I felt how weak I was and realized I was in no condition to undertake a long hike.

"Mama, I cannot go on this march. I know that after a few steps out of the camp I won't be able to keep pace with everybody. I'll fall by the wayside and be shot. I cannot go."

Mother could see it was true.

"You are right, Renia," she said. "We'll just go back."

Fryda also was drained, barely able to walk. So Aunt Andzia and Fryda made the same decision, and all four of us returned to our hospital barrack.

A while later we heard a truck ride through the camp as a guard called over a loudspeaker, "Alle Juden raus! Alle Juden raus!" ordering the remaining prisoners to leave the barracks. I was frightened.

When the truck drove off, we left the hospital barrack to look for a safe hiding place. The four of us searched other barracks till we came upon a deserted one at the end of the camp. We went in through the back entrance and closed the doors behind us. Then we picked up a few wooden boards from a bottom sleeping bunk, which was close to the floor, crawled in, slid the wooden planks back in place so that no one would notice we were hidden there, and lay quietly on the cold floor. Channah Mell from Tomaszow followed us into the barrack but decided not to hide with us. She was hysterical and frantically ran towards the birch woods outside of camp, thinking she would be safer there. But as she ran a guard shot and killed her.

We heard footsteps and repeated screaming of "Alle Juden raus!" followed by shots. Silently we lay, hoping that no one would enter the empty barrack and discover us.

"I remember practically holding my breath. We lay there until it was dark," said Fryda.

At that point all was quiet. We slid out from our hiding place and under cover of darkness returned back to the hospital barrack. Several corpses were sprawled on the white snow.

With no guards around, Mother and Andzia went to the kitchen barrack and brought back some potatoes and cabbage. Andzia used the ingredients to cook soup in a large kettle. Some prisoners cut the wires to gain access to the warehouse and picked clothing for themselves. Mother went also and returned with some blankets, sweaters, a jacket to keep me warm, and a little black suitcase that contained Odol mouthwash.[9]

For the next few days we remained at the hospital barrack, where I occupied the top of a three-tiered bunk, a vantage point from which I observed people in that barrack in the throes of death. I saw one *Muselmann* after another, people who were physically and emotionally exhausted, completely beyond help, those who had just given up on life—their eyes seemed dead—and who were virtually walking corpses. They trudged over to the pile of bodies in the center of the barrack, recognizing that death was near, that their end was just a matter of minutes or hours away, lay down on the pile of Muselmanner, and expired within a short time. It was a horrifying sight.

The bodies were stacked on top of each other, and each day the pile grew. Human bodies with very narrow leg bones, pelvic bones, and rib bones protruding through a thin layer of skin, half-dead people, inhaling their final breaths, barely living skeletons who had lost all will to live.

Several days passed, and we did not see any Germans. Aunt Andzia suggested leaving camp and trying to hide in a nearby town in case the Nazis returned. I put on my newly acquired jacket, and the four of us, Andzia, Fryda, Mother, and I set out on our trail.

Everything was buried under a thick blanket of snow; we could not see the roads, and we did not know which direction to go. Aunt Andzia and Mama brought a stool and a wicker basket to use as sleds for Fryda and me. Before long I was sitting on the inverted stool as Mama pulled me with a rope.

As we walked a hail of bullets began flying from all directions. Frightened, we fell to the ground. We advanced a few steps and hit the ground again as bullets swished above us.

Finally, we crawled from the shower of bullets and continued on our trek. I alternated between walking when I could muster enough energy and sitting on the inverted stool. Finally, before our eyes appeared a gate with the sign "Arbeit Macht Frei" ("work makes you free"). We had reached the main gate of Auschwitz I, the smaller original Auschwitz camp! We walked into the first brick building to find it deserted. There was no point in staying there in the abandoned barracks, so we turned around and walked slowly back to Birkenau (Auschwitz II). It had been a futile, wasted trek.

Back in Birkenau we heard rumblings of guns from a distance, an indication that the front was very near, but we had no idea what the outcome might be.

Then, one morning there was a big commotion. Off in the distance soldiers were approaching.

"These little figures in long coats were tromping across the thigh-deep snow in our direction," remembered Fryda.

Mother and I walked outside to see Russian soldiers entering the camp. Several of the soldiers walked into our barrack and cried upon seeing the horrific condition of the prisoners, those still alive and those who did not survive.

It was January 27, 1945. We had been liberated!

"I remember feeling incredible excitement, huge excitement," said Fryda. "The nightmare was over. We were going to be free people again. It was an incredible feeling."

But I felt neither elation nor even gratitude because I was so sick. I was simply struggling to stay alive.

There was much sadness too. The six long years of Nazi oppression weighed heavily on me: not only the precariousness of my physical condition but also the uncertainty of my father's fate, Romek's murder—he had been gassed and burned in Auschwitz—a painful tragedy with which I had not fully dealt, and the fact that my grandparents and most of my relatives had been killed in Treblinka. I had been liberated, yet I was still surrounded by death.

At least I had my mother, for which I was grateful. And I fervently hoped to be reunited with Papa. I also began to feel valued again, thanks to the Russian soldiers' sympathy for us.

General Vasily Petrenko was the commander of the Red Army that liberated Auschwitz. Forty-seven years later I had the honor of meeting him at a Child Holocaust Survivors Conference in Israel, where I walked over to General Petrenko and expressed in broken Russian my gratitude to him for liberating Auschwitz.

The Polish Red Cross transferred us to the original Auschwitz camp (Auschwitz I), where the brick barracks were better insulated against the cold. We slept on cots rather than three-tiered bunk beds and had thick, warm blankets instead of the threadbare coverings with holes that had provided minimal warmth in Birkenau.

A Russian doctor examined me and prescribed large doses of vitamin C, which Polish Red Cross nurses would dispense as they walked through the barrack. I can still taste the acidic vitamin C tab-

Rena Margulies, Hinda Margulies in Auschwitz. Photo taken by Russians after liberation. Rena is in the center, wearing a uniform she had never worn during imprisonment. Hinda Margulies is in the rear wearing dark clothing. Courtesy of Auschwitz-Birkenau State Museum Archives.

Hinda Margulies in Auschwitz. Photo taken by Russians after liberation. Hinda Margulies is in the center looking at the camera. Courtesy of Auschwitz-Birkenau State Museum Archives.

lets. Though the taste was a bit unpleasant, I was grateful for those vitamins as well as the nutritious food the nurses served us.

One day Russian soldiers with a camera crew came into our barrack at Auschwitz I, asking us to go outside and be filmed to create a record of what had happened to us.

"It is important that the world should see that we were here, what went on here, and that no one came to our rescue till now," said Mama.

The Russians provided striped prisoner uniforms that I had never worn. I put on the uniform over the gray sackcloth dress I had received when I first arrived at Birkenau in July. Mama and some other adults did not receive a uniform. Those who were still mobile were asked to walk between two rows of barbed wires. We did as requested while a cameraman filmed our group. The filmmakers also asked some of us to pull up our sleeves so they could record the tattooed numbers on our left forearms. That film clip was later used in documentaries about the Holocaust. While the film did serve as documentation of our plight, our segment also left the false impression that we had worn prisoner uniforms at Auschwitz-Birkenau.

6: Searching for a New Life

Return to Tomaszow

As soon as I recovered some strength, we left Auschwitz to return to Tomaszow, where we hoped to reunite with Papa and resume our former life. The Polish Red Cross gave us certificates entitling us to free passage to our hometown.

Mama and I, as well as Aunt Andzia and Fryda, left Auschwitz on a Russian army truck to Krakow. There we stayed in a building operated by Jewish survivors who were helping other former prisoners traveling back home. We slept in a very large empty room on straw mattresses laid out on the floor. Mama went to the main market to sell some of the blankets that we had brought with us from camp, and after a week in Krakow, we boarded a packed train to our hometown.

It didn't take long to learn that the war's conclusion had not brought an end to anti-Semitism. Poles on the train, surprised to see Jews who had survived, exclaimed, "There are still Jews alive!" and "Oh, the Jews are back. Too bad that Hitler didn't kill you all." When Aunt Eva returned, she also heard such comments.

At the first stop in Kielce, some Poles shoved Mama and Aunt Andzia off the train. Amid the rush of people pushing to get onboard, the doors closed, preventing Fryda and me from following our mothers. Mama called out, "Wait for me at the Tomaszow train station."

A kind woman saw how anxious we were. She was going to our town and told us, "Stay with me, I'm also getting off at Tomaszow." When we arrived we remained at the railroad station until our mothers came on the very next train.

Walking from the railroad station to the center of town, we saw remnants of destroyed and bombed-out buildings. At our apartment, number 21 Antoniego, we found another family living there. We in-

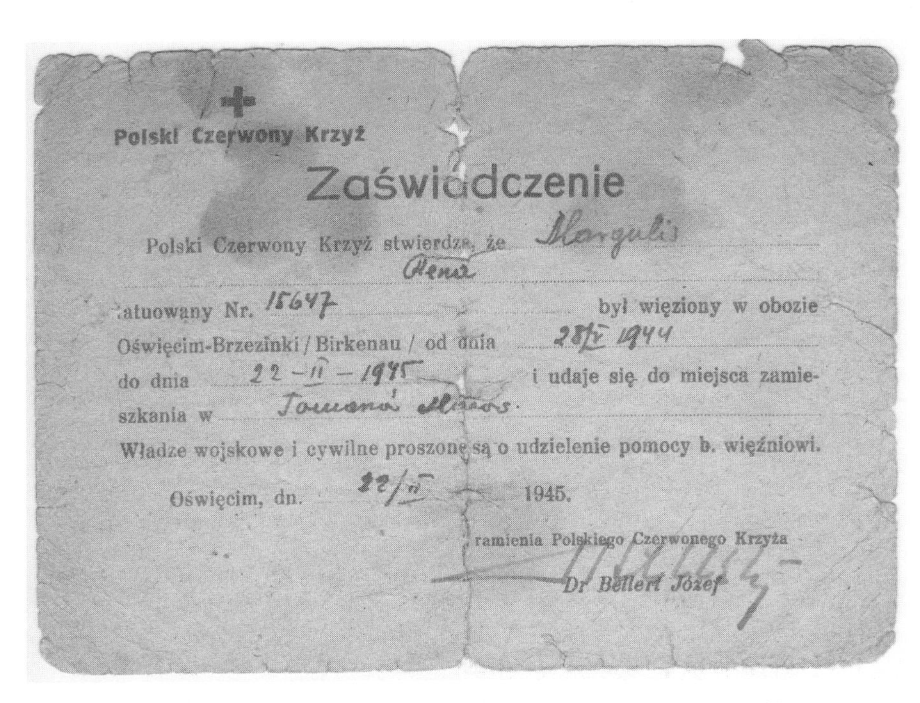

Polski Czerwony Krzyż

Zaświadczenie

Polski Czerwony Krzyż stwierdza, że Margulis Rena

:atuowany Nr. 15647 był więziony w obozie Oświęcim-Brzezinki / Birkenau / od dnia 28/V 1944 do dnia 22 – II – 1945 i udaje się do miejsca zamieszkania w Tomaszów Maz.

Władze wojskowe i cywilne proszone są o udzielenie pomocy b. więźniowi.

Oświęcim, dn. 22/II 1945.

ramienia Polskiego Czerwonego Krzyża

Dr Bellert Józef

Rena Margulies's Polish Red Cross liberation document. Courtesy of Rena Margulies Chernoff.

quired if there were vacant apartments in town and were directed to the apartment that had belonged to Dr. Okno, Aunt Eva's dentist, who had been deported to Treblinka. The German family that had lived there during the war fled when the Russian army liberated Tomaszow. The apartment still had Dr. Okno's furniture, including the white porcelain-topped dentist's desk, some small dental instruments, such as a dentist's mirror, and on the wall hung a painting of Jerusalem's Wailing Wall. Across the painting was written, "Jude Verrecke" ("Jew be destroyed").

For the first several days we went to the public kitchen and stood in line to get food.

Mama now had to earn a livelihood by putting her skills as a dressmaker to use so she needed a sewing machine. After learning that the *Sammelstelle*, the warehouse, still contained some machines the Germans had confiscated, Mama went there and found her old Singer. Aunt Andzia located hers as well. Mama's seamstress skills were in demand, and she soon had a good number of customers.

Meanwhile, we befriended a Jewish woman whose son was stationed in Tomaszow for the Russian army. They were kind and supplied us with all sorts of wonderful food.

Liberation of Other Tomaszowers

As we tried to rebuild a life in Tomaszow, the Allies were reaching other camps where Tomaszowers were imprisoned.

American troops entered Ebensee on May 6, 1945, liberating the concentration camp's prisoners, including Uncle Jozef. Hundreds of prisoners lay around the camp, many dead, others swollen from starvation. Some of those who were still physically able immediately exacted retribution from the camp's tailor Kappo and shoe Kappo, forcing them into a lake and then stoning them to death.

It was the British army that liberated Aunt Eva along with Mania Warzecha, Rose Szyk, and Cousin Hanka Lew at Bergen-Belsen on April 15, 1945.

Disease and malnutrition were rampant through the overcrowded camp. Tragically, the Brits did not know how to properly nurse the thousands of starved prisoners, feeding them regular army rations of pork and beans, which caused dysentery to break out in the camp. One of every five prisoners at Bergen-Belsen, more than 13,000 people, died shortly after liberation.[1]

"It was poison for our people," said Hanka. "I got sick in Bergen-Belsen. I couldn't pick up a piece of bread. . . . I don't know how we survived. It's beyond me."

Even so, Cousin Hanka did live.

"I had the hope! I hoped and prayed we will survive," recalled Hanka. "Stronger people than me died."

Also liberated at Bergen-Belsen was Wolf Kaiser. From there he went to a displaced persons (D.P.) camp in the German town of Celle, near Hannover. Administrators there immediately tried to change the former prisoners' self-image. Kaiser said they uncovered German depots filled with military uniforms, most from the Luftwaffe, and had the freed Jews wear the clean uniforms to replace their striped prisoner garb. As they walked through Celle, townspeople approached Kaiser and his friends, asking in which military unit they had served.

Liberation did not come easy for the many thousands of prisoners the Nazis had forced on death marches as they evacuated the camps.

Fishel Samelson was on a march out of Birkenau on January 18, 1945, as the Nazis were busy trying to clear out the Auschwitz-Birkenau complex where Mama and I had remained. His group of 130 men trudged for several days through the snow until they came to a train that took them to Gross-Rosen. When they arrived Fishel saw prisoners being beaten and decided he wouldn't be able to survive the camp.

"So [we] just got on a line. We didn't know what the line was for. And that line was shipped out to Dachau," said Fishel.

Samelson and his friends, Icher Cymberg, Itzek Biderman, and Henry Mellen, were at the Dachau camp for several days, then sent to Mühldorf, a Dachau subcamp about forty miles northeast of Munich. There they worked in a quarry, a *Steinbruch*, breaking up stones supposedly for use in constructing concealed airplane hangars.

One day they were placed on a train headed toward the Tyrolean Mountains. The train stopped near Seeshaupt, thirty miles southwest of Munich. After a long wait Fishel checked and found there were no Germans aboard. Apparently they had fled.

"Henry said, 'It would be good to smuggle into the village. Maybe I'll be able to find a potato or something,'" remembered Fishel. "He did smuggle out and he went into town and the town is only twenty minutes away. And here is one hour, two hours, three hours, and he hasn't come back. We started to worry. He might have been caught and God knows what happened. And this was already late in the afternoon. [Then] we see a body approaching from a distance, and I said to the other guys, 'Someone's coming.'

"Sure enough, he came back. Mellen, he walked like this with a handful of oranges and chocolate and white bread and drinks. I said 'Where are you from? Heaven?' He said 'No. You see over there,' he says. 'That's the American tanks.' And that's how we were liberated."

On May 1, 1945, Szmul and Leibish Szampaner were reunited after they had briefly met each other in Birkenau. But it was a grim reunion since they were both trudging on a death march from Kaufering to Allach, two Dachau subcamps in the northwestern outskirts of Munich.

"For surviving, no one was thinking," remembered Szmul.

When the sounds of shots were heard, Szmul and his brother ducked into the woods, escaping the march.

"I was running in the woods and running in the woods, and we saw all of a sudden a tank came in, an American tank," said Szmul. "I never saw such a big tank."

Szmul and Leibish climbed to freedom on board the tank and were welcomed by its Polish-American captain. Immediately the American crew provided much-needed nourishment for the Szampaner brothers.

"They gave us food on the tank. They gave us white bread. I never saw white bread [before]," marveled Szmul.

The brothers arrived in Starnberg, Germany, where Leibush told a Polish-speaking lieutenant, "I'd like to work for the company [of soldiers]." The Americans appropriated sewing machines and provided Leibish and Szmul a room in a local hotel where they sewed Eisenhower jackets (cut very short) and pants for the American troops.

"They treated me well," said Leibush. "They gave us a motorcycle."

When the U.S. army company moved to Landsburg, the Szampaners came along, continuing to sew for the soldiers.

Search for Survivors

After liberation, the thoughts of all Tomaszowers turned to loved ones. Were they were still alive? Where might they be found? A pan-European dash ensued as survivors hunted for *mishpocha* (family) and landsleit (fellow townsfolk). Husbands and wives sought each other. Those who were single or recently widowed searched for a partner, someone with whom they could rebuild a new life.

Szmul Szampaner went to Bergen-Belsen to bring Sala Kenigsztejn to Landsberg. Soon Szmul and Sala were married. Sala's friend Mania Markowicz came along to Landsberg as well, where she would marry Leibish.

Fishel Samelson and Kathy Miller were on the same transport train bound for the Tyrolean Mountains that stopped at Seeshaupt. After American troops liberated the prisoners, they provided housing for them in town, which is where Fishel and Kathy met. In January of 1946, the two were married.

Aunt Eva heard that her husband Meylekh was at St. Otillien Archabbey, a Benedictine monastery where some survivors were housed and receiving care. She traveled across Germany, riding on top of trains, to reach St. Otillien, in Eresing, Germany, twenty-nine miles west of Munich.

"I arrived in St. Otillien, I was disappointed. There were some people who were in the same camp as my husband. They said he passed away . . . starved to death," said Eva.

Meylekh had been a chain smoker. Too often in Auschwitz he traded his little piece of daily bread for cigarettes.

Back in Munich Aunt Eva met Tomaszower Avram Shmuel (Abe) Romanowitz.

Avram Shmuel's wife and two children had been deported to Treblinka with most of Tomaszow's Jews where they were murdered.

"He said, 'What are you going to do?'" remembered Eva.

"So I said, 'I'm going back to Poland because I know my sister with her daughter are in Poland and I have to be with them.'"

"Abe said, 'I go too.'"

"So I said, 'Whom do you have? What for are you going?'"

"'I go.' he said. So he went," recounted Eva.

They married on April 23, 1946. There was no way to bring back the dead, and life had to go on.

After their liberation from the Theresienstadt camp and ghetto, Cousin Rutka, Zlacia Warzecha, her sister Frymcia, and Genia Rozanski arrived at the Red Cross center in Prague, about forty miles away, where they met four men from Tomaszow searching for family.

"They said my sister Anna is already in Tomaszow and Fryda as well as Renia and Hinda," said Zlacia. "So we went right away on the train. We didn't have any money; we didn't have anything. We were traveling on top of the train."

Sitting not far behind the smokestack they were smothered with soot from the coal-operated train. "We came in dirty to town. They sent us right away to a public bath," said Zalcia.

As Tomaszowers returned to town they would inquire, "Where do the Jews live?" Invariably, the Poles would direct them to our apartment, which was essentially the official greeting office and guest house for Tomaszowers who had survived the camps, hidden in cellars, in attics, in barns, in convents, and with the partisans in forests. Some had constantly been on the run. Some escaped to Russia, and others survived on false papers.

Aunt Eva arrived with Abe. Cousin Chemja Tenenbaum came

Frymcia Warzecha, Zlacia Warzecha, and Genia Rozanski (front to back) in Tomaszow shortly after the war. Courtesy of Zlacia Warzecha.

back from Russia. We heard that Hanka had also survived and was still in Germany after her liberation from Bergen-Belsen.

Every day I waited for news about my father with hope for his return. As time went by dozens of people came back but not Papa, which heightened my anxiety about his fate. As each Tomaszower arrived, Mama posed questions: "How did you survive? Where were you? With whom were you? Did you see my husband, Avram Chaim Margulies?"

Then one day we heard that Mr. Aaron Cukierman, who had been with my father in the camps, had made his way back to Tomaszow. Mother and I went to his apartment to hear news about the whereabouts of Papa. Cukierman related to us that he was with Papa in Auschwitz, before being sent on a transport. In December 1944 he met my father again in Camp Ohrdruf near the town of Gotha, Germany. In late March 1945 they were together on a transport. Then, in early May 1945, Mr. Cukierman said, he and my father were on a death march in a small village, Freilassing, near Germany's southeastern border with Austria. Papa and four other men tried to escape the march, but as they hid an SS man shot and killed Papa on May 6, 1945, one day before liberation.

I was completely stunned and could hardly believe it. I had been hoping against all odds that that my father was still alive, that he might eventually show up, as others had.

Papa was such a vibrant person, full of life. He was good and loving. He helped out people with whatever he could and he saved fellow Tomaszowers and relatives during the war.

In spite of Cukierman's eyewitness account, it took me a long

OFFICE OF LIAISON AND SECURITY FOR LK SCHWABMUNCHEN
APO 407 US ARMY

Director/GHW/rg

9 July 1947

C E R T I F I C A T E

It is hereby certified that the tailor shop Medrich of Schwabmunchen, Feyerabendstrasse 5, has passed into the hands of the firm Samulewitz Josef, Rosanski Israel and Russak Nathan all living in Schwabmunchen in the month of August 1945 by order of Military Government. Mr. Russak has relinquished his share in the above mentioned firm on 1 June 1947. At present the firm operates under the name of Samulewitz - Rosanski.

George H. Waters
GEORGE H WATERS
Capt INF
Director

U.S. military authorization letter for Josef Zamulewicz and Israel "Srulek" Rozanski to operate a tailor shop in Schwabmunchen after the war. Courtesy of Josef Zamulewicz.

time to come to terms with the fact that my father would not be found somewhere in the maelstrom of people traveling, looking for members of their families after the war. Eventually I realized that if he had not shown up after several years, then he was indeed dead. He loved his family, and he would have surfaced had he been alive. Still, in my heart of hearts I could not fully accept the death of my dear father, and I did not start grieving for Tatus as well as Romek till many years later.

Mother was totally devastated with the news of her husband's death. Now she had to be both a mother and a father to me.

Heartache came to others who failed to reunite with loved ones. Frieda Szajewicz's family had made a plan prior to the evacuation of Tomaszow—that they would meet at their grandfather's grave in the cemetery if they were separated. After the war she returned there with her sister. Though she had found her brother's clothing while sorting property for the Nazis at Tomaszow's Sammelstelle, clear evidence that he had been deported to the Treblinka death camp along with most of Tomaszow's Jews, Frieda still had a shred of faith that somehow he might have survived.

"We had hoped maybe someone would be there," said Frieda.

But when no one from the family arrived in Tomaszow, she and her sister knew that indeed they were the only survivors.

Poles had taken the family's apartment. "They said they had sent money to Auschwitz for it," said Frieda. Soon the sisters left for a Displaced Persons camp in Germany.

Some surviving Tomaszowers did not return to town, never wanting to go back, including Josef Zamulewicz, who stayed in Schwabmünchen, Germany, west of Munich.

"I went up to the American officer. I said, 'I'm a tailor. I would like to work.' So he went to where there was a Nazi-run tailor shop. He said, 'You take this over.' Then he gave me a permit," said Josef.

In Tomaszow I joined a library and read voraciously, hungry for knowledge that I lacked and motivated to catch up for the more than five years of formal learning I had missed. In September 1945 I enrolled in fifth grade at the Polish public school and did well despite having missed all those years of education.

Fryda also attended the public school. But the other children made us feel like we did not belong. We sat while the Polish stu-

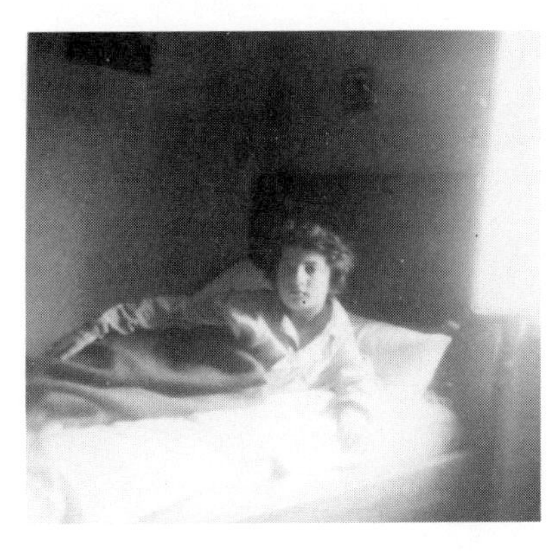

Rena Margulies back in Tomaszow, still weak after liberation from Birkenau. Courtesy of Fryda Tenenbaum.

dents stood to say their daily prayers and were in class but did not participate while a nun taught religion. A private Jewish tutor instructed me in religion at home.

At dismissal time several Polish students chased after us, throwing stones.

"Jew. Dirty Jew. Smelly Jew. Get out of here," Fryda remembered the aggressors yelling.

As soon as the bell rang, we ran home as fast as we could to avoid being hit. Our mothers went to the principal and complained. Thereafter, Fryda and I were dismissed a few minutes earlier so that we could rush home safely.

One day Mama and Aunt Eva went over to their parents' house on Bozniczna Street. But the little wooden ranch house that had belonged to Grandma Raizel and Grandpa Hershel Tenenbaum was gone; it had been razed. All that remained was a vacant field covered with grass and the seckel pear tree that had stood by the house. Mama, with Eva's help, dug in the area where she and Papa had buried their bales of fabrics, but they found nothing. Someone had combed through the soil and taken all that had been hidden there.

There was nothing holding us back from leaving Tomaszow. Our home was no longer there, our family had perished, and anti-Semitism was rampant, having only grown during the war years. The life we had known in our hometown was indeed gone forever. Recalling the address of our family in the United States, Mama wrote a letter to Aunt Susie (Zisel) Rosenberg in Brooklyn, New York, who urged us to emigrate.

Ironically, the presence of Allied troops in Germany, who controlled the country after the war, made the birthplace of Nazism a far more hospitable place for Jews than Polish cities like Tomaszow. Consequently, once reunited with any surviving family, Tomaszow's Jews left.

It wasn't easy to get out, though. Under Polish government regulations we were not permitted to simply leave the country; borders were tightly controlled. So we had to smuggle out.

Uncle Jozef departed before us, hiring a Russian army officer for whom he had sewn a leather coat to help his family cross the border into Germany. On May Day, May 1, 1946, figuring that the border guards would be drunk that night, Jozef and his wife Andzia wore uniforms to appear as servants of the officer, who was able to drive them and Fryda across the border into Berlin.

"We were squished together. We had one suitcase," said Fryda. "I was in the middle. I had to put my feet out the window. That's how we crossed the border."

The officer left Fryda and her parents in the Russian sector of Berlin. From there they took a street car to the American Zone, where there was a transition camp for displaced persons, Schlachtensee. Then they moved to other D.P. camps, Feldafing, and finally Heidenheim, where there was an apartment for the family.

The following month, once the school year had ended, Mama and I, along with Eva and Abe, departed Tomaszow on a train for Szczecin, Poland, east of Tomaszow, near the German border. Our cousin, Chemja Tenenbaum, who had survived the war in Russia, accompanied us. In Szczecin we stayed several days with Moisio Faigeles, who had moved there from Tomaszow and used his contacts to arrange for a Russian smuggler to transport us to the American Zone in Berlin.

The smuggler, a Russian soldier, drove a canvas-covered military truck so packed with people seeking to cross the border that some passengers had to stand, holding on to the iron framework supporting the truck's canvas cover. We left in the middle of the night. As we approached the border checkpoint the driver accelerated and sped by the sentry to avoid inspection.

"Stop! Stop!" yelled the guards. Then they began shooting. A bullet pierced the arm of a man standing above me, and blood began trickling onto my face. I didn't think much of it. I had seen far worse.

Several hours later we arrived in Berlin's Schlachtensee neighborhood.

Heidenheim Castle on the hill. Courtesy of Fryda Tenenbaum.

We had not left Poland too soon. Pogroms against Jews resumed, including an infamous one in Kielce—the town where our mothers had been thrown off the train—resulting in the death of forty-two Jews.

After registering with the authorities at the Schlachtensee D.P. camp we received food, clothing, and accommodations in barracks specially constructed for refugees. I even attended school for the few weeks we spent there, from June 19 to August 7, 1946.

But it was the beginning of a difficult period of adjustment for me. For the prior five years—normally an important period of development—I had been severely deprived, starved, enslaved, and a witness to torture and mass murder. I felt I was bereft of virtually everything.

Walking Schlachtensee's peaceful streets I saw lovely small houses, well maintained, surrounded by gardens with blooming flowers. It seemed they had been untouched by the war. While Nazis had tormented and massacred other human beings, their families had lived in comfortable homes like these.

In August we left Schlachtensee and went to another displaced persons camp in Heidenheim, Germany, located on the site of an old settlement for employees of a local factory, where accommodations were more comfortable. Mama and I were assigned one room and shared kitchen facilities with three other families living in the same one-family house: Eva and Abe; Frymcia Warzecha and Srulek Markowicz from Tomaszow, who had married by then, as well as my D.P. camp Hebrew teacher and her husband.

I learned much in Heidenheim from teachers in the camp's school, as well as from private tutors who taught Fryda and me algebra, geometry, chemistry, physics, French, and English, among other subjects.

I even had several friends. Two girls from Vilna, Lithuania—Frieda Bernstein and Tamar Ginsburg, who had escaped to Russia during the war—bonded with Fryda and myself. What made our friendship particularly interesting was the fact that they spoke only Russian and Yiddish. So Fryda and I, raised in Polish-speaking households by parents who knew Yiddish, were forced to finally learn decent Yiddish.

Heidenheim was a picture-postcard village with a small zoo and an old castle on a hill that served as a theater for puppet plays and other shows. Residents meticulously manicured their flower gar-

Classroom in Heidenheim D.P. Camp, Rena and Fryda in rear. Courtesy of Fryda Tenenbaum.

(Left to right) Rena Margulies, Frieda Bernstein, and Fryda Tenenbaum in Heidenheim. Courtesy of Fryda Tenenbaum.

Rena and Fryda in Heidenheim. Courtesy of Fryda Tenenbaum.

Heidenheim Lag B'Omer celebration. Eretz Yisrael banner. Courtesy of Fryda Tenenbaum.

dens. Stores were stocked with all kinds of merchandise, and the movie house showed the latest productions.

"It looked as if the war had not happened there. And that was a bitter feeling that these people had lived normal lives. There was no bomb damage. There was no destruction," said Fryda. "Sometimes we would go into town and go to a movie, and that was always very difficult in terms of the interactions with the people," she added. "The trauma was fresh and just being in a German place and hearing German spoken was incredibly difficult."

Bars were filled with Germans drinking mugs of beer, laughing and enjoying a very pleasant, comfortable life. Many of them had been Nazi Party members and perhaps participants in the Nazi atrocities. Inside I was filled with anger, just as I had felt in Schlachtensee. As I looked at those people, I hated them for what they had done to us. The fact that they could go scot-free while we had lost our family and were dispossessed of everything we had owned further infuriated me. Only my awareness that I could be arrested for hurting any of them prevented me from acting upon my fury.

Meanwhile, my personal identity to Judaism grew. Not only did I attend Hebrew school, but I also joined a Zionist group, which built my bond with Palestine. I was ready to move to the Holy Land. Our group even practiced jujitsu in preparation for meeting pioneer challenges in Palestine. Mama, though, had other plans.

In Heidenheim she married Jakub Wolard. While Jakub would never replace Papa for either of us, he was a good man, a Tomaszower tailor who had also suffered the loss of his first spouse and his child, and under the circumstances, a reliable partner. Mama and Jakub applied for American immigration papers. So I kept my thoughts of aliyah to myself, not having the temerity to share my feelings with them.

Fryda also was prepared to make aliyah to Palestine, but her parents also had their sights set on the United States. The number of immigrants permitted into the United States was limited under quotas so we had to wait patiently.

Visas to emigrate arrived for Fryda and her parents as well as for Eva and Avram Shmuel. Both families departed on ships for America in March of 1949.

Fryda traveled on a converted troop carrier ship, the *SS Marine Jumper*, which docked in Boston. From there she and her parents boarded a train for New York.

"On the train platform Red Cross ladies gave out hot chocolate and doughnuts. It was nice," said Fryda. "I remember getting on the train. I was sitting at the window and down along the sides of the track was trash and rusty machinery. As the train pulled out of Boston, I thought, this is America? Then we arrived at Grand Central Station, which was very elegant. I remember staring at the marble staircase in Grand Central."

Seven months later it was our turn. So, after three years in Heidenheim, we left the displaced persons camp for the port city of Bremerhaven, West Germany. There, after receiving a medical examination, we were permitted to leave for the United States. In October of 1949, just over ten years after the beginning of the war that had destroyed our lives and our families, Mama, Jakub, and I departed onboard the *USS General Harry Taylor* for a new life in the United States.

It was a solid military ship, but once we were at sea I could feel constant rocking, a sensation I had never experienced. When we sat

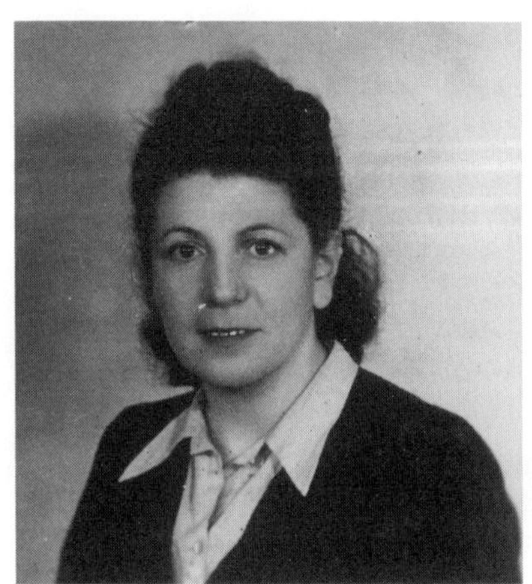

Hinda Tenebaum Margulies, now Hinda Wolard in Heidenheim. Courtesy of Fryda Tenenbaum.

Jakub Wolard in Heidenheim. Courtesy of Rena Margulies Chernoff.

New Year's card from Jakub, Rena, and Hinda. Courtesy of Rena Margulies Chernoff.

to eat, plates on the dining-room table slid from side to side. I felt like one of those plates as I lay in my berth. Such constant swaying made me seasick, and I vomited through most of the trip. As we approached New York Harbor on October 13, 1949, everyone gathered on the deck to view the Statue of Liberty, the highlight of our cross-Atlantic voyage, but I was so exhausted that I slept.

Once we passed through immigration inspection, Aunt Susie and her family embraced us warmly. She took Mama and Jakub, now "Jacob" or "Jack" under his new Americanized spelling, to her home in Brooklyn, and cousins Gerri and Al Rosenberg drove me to their house in Forest Hills, Queens. After recovering from the journey I was thrilled to finally be in the United States, and to have received such a gracious welcome from our American cousins, for which I was extremely appreciative.

The very next day Gerri brought me to Forest Hills High School, where I enrolled. The principal asked me to solve several mathematics problems, but he could not test me in English subjects because I lacked command of the language. Still, he decided to place me in the junior class, which was the appropriate grade for my age, sixteen.

I sat through most subjects not fully understanding what the teacher was saying, trying to infer the lesson, unsure whether or not my interpretation was correct. Mathematics was far easier because I could follow the examples without needing to understand every single English word.

A Place of My Own

While I remained with Gerri and Al, Aunt Susie found housing for Mama, Jacob, Aunt Eva, Uncle Abe, and Hershel (Hershie), their two-month-old son born in August, first a temporary apartment, and several weeks later, a permanent one on Troy Avenue in Brooklyn.

Housing was in such short supply that the landlord required "key money" for the apartment and its used furniture, $2,000—a huge sum at the time. We had arrived penniless in the United States, but our relatives proved invaluable. One by one they contributed until Aunt Susie collected the required amount.

The railroad-style apartment at 259 Troy Avenue had six rooms, and one of them, facing the street, was mine! I was elated to finally have a room of my own and asked Mother to have it painted green, my favorite color. As soon as it was painted, I left Gerri and Al's house in Forest Hills and moved in with Mama and Jack in Brooklyn.

It was still the middle of the term at Forest Hills High School, so I had to travel an hour each way by subway from Brooklyn to Queens every school day until the end of the semester. Unaccustomed to riding the subway, again I suffered from motion sickness, vomiting daily on the train. Fortunately, the following semester I transferred to Tilden High School in Brooklyn.

As I studied, the Tomaszow tailors who had utilized their sewing skills to survive the war now put those talents to use to earn a living. Jack found a job in Manhattan's Garment District, working as a tailor for a company called Shotland Modes, which, among other things, designed and manufactured uniforms for American Airlines. Nuta—now Nathan—Romer and Uncle Jozef—now Joe—landed jobs there as well. The Tomaszowers, as new immigrants, took particular pride in creating uniforms for AMERICAN Airlines.

Eva visited well-to-do customers, bringing home their garments, which she would alter to earn money. Eventually she would also join Shotland Modes, working as a seamstress.

Years later Uncle Joe would work at some of the biggest designer houses in Manhattan's Garment Center—Hattie Carnegie, Elizabeth Arden, and Oscar de la Renta.

Srulek Rozanski, who had worked for my father, and Josef Zamulewicz—now Joseph Samuels—went into business together, opening a tailor shop on Manhattan's Upper West Side at 74th Street and Broadway. Fishel Samelson and Genia Rozanski crafted classic American garments for the men's apparel firm J. Press. Szmul Szampaner, who changed his name to Sam Shampain, and his brother Leibish, who became Leon Shampaner, also sewed in New York's bustling garment business.

Learning the trade of tailoring had been a practical step in prewar Poland, where career options for Jews were severely restricted. Tailoring also proved to be a lifesaving profession for all of these Tomaszowers, and in America, our new country, it was now providing the means for them to rebuild their lives.

Papa's tailoring talent had allowed him to save the lives of other Tomaszowers. It nearly did the same for him, but tragically his life was cut short. While Mama did survive the war, she was too ill to work in the United States, so she cooked for us all and gave loving care to Hershie while Eva was at work.

In Tomaszow every year at Grandma Raizel's Passover seder we recited the story of the ancient Hebrews' exodus from slavery in Egypt for which we gave thanks to God.

Millennia later, the Jews of Europe had been slaves and worse—victims of a mass murder extermination campaign that wiped out six million human lives, including those of my father, brother, grandparents, cousins, neighbors, and friends. I was fortunate to have been part of a modern exodus from slavery and a horrific oppressor. As we sat at Aunt Susie's Passover table in the spring of 1950 for our first celebration of the holiday in the United States, I was filled with gratitude. Brooklyn was not the biblical Promised Land, not the pioneer environment I had embraced and prepared myself for as a teenager in postwar Europe. But Brooklyn, USA, was a blessed, welcoming refuge, a safe home, and a place of permanence where I could build a life.

7: Afterward

In January 1951 I graduated from Tilden High School, took the admissions exam for Brooklyn College, and began my studies there the very next month. While attending Brooklyn College I worked twice-a-week, four-hour shifts, as a bookkeeper at a wholesale distribution center in Brooklyn that delivered candies to candy stores. The experience reinforced my determination to attend and graduate from college so my horizons would be expanded beyond being a store clerk.

Meanwhile, Mama's health declined. When she arrived in the United States, her rectal cancer was dormant, but soon it relapsed and spread. She endured severe pain, and I would give her injections of Demerol to ease her suffering. The doctors at Memorial Hospital and James Ewing Hospital in Manhattan could do only so much. On June 14, 1954, Mama passed away.

I took her death very hard. Because I had not grieved for my brother or father, my mourning now for Mama also included Romek and Papa. I felt alone in my grief.

As much pain as Mama's death brought, I knew I had to move forward and begin a career. In February of 1955, I graduated from Brooklyn College with a degree in economics and immediately started work in Manhattan at the Hill and Knowlton public relations firm as an economic researcher, focusing primarily on the economics of the steel industry. While working, I pursued my masters degree in economics at New York University. Eventually I would become an elementary school teacher, specializing in remedial mathematics. Since I had missed so much of my childhood, being able to work with children was especially gratifying for me.

I continued to live at Troy Avenue with Aunt Eva, Abe, and Hershie, contributing to household expenses. (Jacob had moved out to remarry.) During summer weekends I rented a room in a boarding house by the beach in Far Rockaway, where I made friends and enjoyed an active social life.

While it appeared that I had adjusted well, inside I realized that I still had many unresolved issues. My years of persecution and incarceration in the Tomaszow ghetto, Blizyn labor camp, and the Auschwitz-Birkenau concentration camp had a deep impact. I had lost my father, my brother, my grandparents, as well as much of my extended family, and I missed them dearly. To avoid any further calamity or persecution I became very self-protective, almost withdrawing into an inner shell. Not knowing how to move past my trauma, I was stuck in a state of limbo. I also had problems with decision making, going in mental circles when it came to important choices. I received several proposals of marriage, but I had a terrible time deciding, leading me to reject my suitors. A friend from high school told me about her psychiatrist, Dr. Simon Rothenberg, who was helping her address personal problems, and I decided to get psychological help as well.

Dr. Rothenberg was a wonderful doctor. I visited his office in Brooklyn once a week for several years. He helped with the process of grieving, which allowed me to put my trauma behind, lower my guard, and become more trusting and decisive. Aunt Eva was a great source of support as my sounding board.

In 1957 I married Benjamin Chernoff, a handsome chemical engineer whom I had met at a dance at Columbia University, where he was studying part-time for his masters degree. We didn't discuss my Holocaust experience very much, but Ben was always very supportive.

The truth is I simply didn't talk much about the Holocaust with anyone. My children, Allan and Helen (born in 1959 and 1961, respectively), knew that I had survived Auschwitz—they saw the tattoo on my forearm every day—but as they grew I hardly discussed it with them, not wanting to burden them with any of my trauma, nor with the weight of the Holocaust itself.

Not until I attended a survivors' convention, the American Gathering of Jewish Holocaust Survivors in Washington, DC, in 1980 did I finally begin to open up about my experience and share it more with the children. While I had known and even socialized with several dozen of the 250 or so surviving Tomaszowers, I had always felt there was a divide between us, a generation gap. Aside from Fryda, who lived in Boston, miles from my home in Brooklyn, virtually all of them were of the older generation since there were so few child survivors and hardly any from Tomaszow. Attending that Washington conference made me feel that I was not alone, that many others had suffered as I had. I learned to speak about my feelings without fear.

Years later I would join Fryda (now Frieda) in Boston with several other Auschwitz child survivors for an annual celebration to mark our liberation from the death camp on January 27, which we considered the day of our rebirth. "Happy Birthday!" we would wish each other, then spend a weekend of bonding, sharing tears and laughter, flowers, food, and drink. Together we explored our tragic past and in so doing helped each other heal.

Eventually I actually became quite vocal in sharing my experience, speaking at many schools, elementary through high school, giving students a firsthand account of what it was like to live through the Holocaust. I appeared on CBS News and CNN and in retirement became a docent at New York's Museum of Jewish Heritage—A Living Memorial to the Holocaust, giving tours of exhibits to school groups.

I never admitted the huge impact the Holocaust had on me. For many years I felt that it was best to forget about it and go on with life. Because I had a mother who shielded me from much of the suffering, I always believed that I was affected less than other Holocaust survivors. I'm sure that is true, but enduring the camps and losing my father, brother, and grandparents left a mark. I did feel pain. The truth is, the grief for survivors never disappears; it merely recedes. Sixty-nine years after liberation at Birkenau, I still carry pain that cannot be erased, even as I am grateful for my blessings, particularly my family and the life of freedom I found in America.

Appendix A

Names of Tomaszowers

Relatives of Rena (Renia) Margulies: (only those cited in the text are listed; numerous more perished in the Holocaust)

Father: Avram Chaim Margulies
Grandparents (parents of Avram Chaim): Rivka Jung & Reuben Margulies
Great-grandparents (parents of Rivka Jung): Shlomo & Simcha Bina Jung
Mother: Hinda (Helen) Tenenbaum Margulies
Grandparents (parents of Hinda): Raizel Kozlowska & Hersh Tenenbaum
Brother: Romek (Reuven) Margulies

Relatives on Mother's (Hinda's) side:

Uncle (brother of Hinda): Josef (Joseph, Joe) Tenenbaum, married to Andzia Warzecha
Cousins (children of Josef & Andzia): Fryda Tenenbaum, Dorka Tenenbaum
Sisters of Andzia Warzecha: Zlacia Warzecha, Frymcia Warzecha, Mania Warzecha
Aunt (sister of Hinda): Eva Tenenbaum
—married to Meylekh Plachta
—married to Avrum Shmuel Romanowitz (Abe Romanowitz)
Cousin: Hershel "Hershie" Romanowitz (son of Eva & Avrum Shmuel)
Aunt (sister of Hinda): Rivka Tenenbaum (moved to Argentina), married to Mordechai Hersz Tenenbaum
Uncle (brother of Hinda): Zalman Icio (moved to Argentina)

Other relatives on Mother's side:

Hinda's aunt: Pearl Golda, married to Moshe Torem
Cousins (children of Pearl Golda & Moshe): Jakub Torem, Gucia Torem, Zosia Torem
Hinda's aunt: Chana, married to Joel Weisbard
Cousins (children of Chana & Joel): Edzia Weisbard, Lola Weisbard, Mania Weisbard
Hinda's cousin Chemja Tenenbaum (employee of Avram Chaim)
Hinda's cousin Hershel Tenenbaum
Hinda's aunt in New York: Zisl (Susie) Kozlowska, married to Israel Machel Rosenberg
Cousins: Al (son of Susie & Israel Machel) & Gerri (Al's wife) Rosenberg
Hinda's uncle in Detroit: Isaac Tenenbaum

Relatives on Father's (Avram Chaim's) side:

Avram Chaim's Aunt Pesa, married to Ichak Lew
Cousins (children of Pesa & Ichak): Hanka (Chana) Lew, Rutka (Rachel) Lew
Avram Chaim's Aunt Ruchel (Rachel), married to Szaja Cwilich
Cousins (children of Rachel & Szaja): Chana Cwilich, Fraidel Cwilich, Bina Cwilich
Avram Chaim's Aunt Chaja, married to Avrum Szychter
Cousins (children of Chaja & Avrum): Shlomo Szychter, Maier Szychter, Simcha Bina (Sabinka) Szychter
Avram Chaim's Uncle Avrum (Avremele Shochet) Jung, married to Miriam
Cousin Pola Margulies

Other Tomaszowers quoted:

Machel Grossman
Wolf Kaiser
Sala Kenigsztejn
Shia (Stephan) Rajzbaum (Sam Reisbaum)
Rose Reizbaum
Nuto (Nathan) Romer (married to Mania Warzecha)
Genia Rozanski
Srulek (Israel) Rozanski (Avram Chaim's apprentice)
Fishel (Felix) Samelson

Nacia Shulmeister
Frieda Szajewicz
Leibish Szampaner (Leon Shampaner)
Szmul (Sam) Szampaner (Sam Shampain)
Josef Zamulewicz (Joseph Samuels) (married to Zlacia Warzecha)

Other Tomaszowers cited in the text:

Employees of Avram Chaim (non-relatives):
- Chamul Belzycki
- Avrum Gersztein (married Hanka Lew)
- Binem Grossman
- Itzhak Hun
- Smil Rozenberg

Avraham Bas (wedding fiddlers)
Dr. Berliner and son Jurek (neighbors)
Cham Burech (neighbor of grandparents)
Chavele Naar ("Eva the fool," candy peddler)
Moisio Faigeles (helped smuggle Rena and family to Berlin)
Franciszka (washer woman)
Zelig Lask
Josef Marshalik (wedding singer)
Marysia (Renia's nanny)
Rudele (grocery-store owner)
Yaakove Shaul
Bolek Szteinman
Jakub Wolard (married Hinda Margulies after the war)
Masha Wolard (first wife of Jakub Wolard)

In Birkenau-Auschwitz:

Bunkmates in Birkenau-Auschwitz:
- Fela Samelson
- Dora Samelson
- Lola Samelson
- Genia Drzazga

Dr. Maniusia Hanel
Mania Markowicz
Channa Mell
Rose Szyk

In Plaszow, Wieliczka & Melk:

Srulek Markowicz
Chaim Modrewski

In Dachau & Muehldof:

Itzek Biderman
Aaron Cukierman
Icher Cymberg
Henry Mellen

Appendix B

Dates of Interviews with Survivors:

(All interviews in person unless otherwise noted. English-Americanized name/married name in parenthesis.)

Motkeh (Mordechai) Berger (Murray Berger): September 10, 1995.
Czeslaw Cyniak: May 4, 1994.
Jakub (Jake) Eisenstein: June 29, 2012 (telephone).
Lazar Grejs: interviewed by Danuta Czech, at Auschwitz-Birkenau Library, June 3, 1986.
Tola Grossman (Tova Friedman): November 8, 1998; November 22, 1998.
Marion Halski: May 1, 1994.
Maniusia Hanel (Maniusia Halski): May 1, 1994.
Hersh Lieb (Herman) Jeruzalski: November 7, 1996 (telephone); November 14, 1996.
Regina Jeruzalski: November 7, 1996 (telephone); November 14, 1996.
Sala Kenigsztejn (Sally Shampain): October 21, 1996; October 24, 1996; December 4, 1996.
Hanka Lew (Hanah Korn): September 22, 1996.
Rutka Lew (Rachel Eisen): August 8, 1992.
Sala Majerowicz (Sally Reisbaum): August 2, 1998; September 27, 1998.
Mania Markowicz (Mary Shampaner): October 21, 1996; October 28, 1996.
Rose Obarzanek (Rose Eisenstein): June 29, 2012 (telephone).
Michal Piasecki: May 1, 1994.
Shia (Stephan) Rajzbaum (Sam Reisbaum): August 2, 1998; September 27, 1998.

Rose (Rachel) Reizbaum: November 17, 1996.
Irka Romer: May 4, 1994.
Nuta (Nathan) Romer: October 1, 1995.
Genia Rozanski (Genia Kuc): November 10, 1996.
Srulek (Israel) Rozanski: January 10, 1998.
Fishel (Felix) Samelson: November 18, 1996; November 19, 1996.
Nacia Schulmeister (Naomi Steinman): November 24, 1996.
Frieda Szajewicz (Franya Freidenreich): October 25, 1996.
Leibish Szampaner (Leon Shampaner): October 21, 1996, October 28, 1996.
Szmul Szampaner (Sam Shampain): October 21, 1996; October 24, 1996; October 31, 1996; December 4, 1996.
Chemja Tenenbaum: August 3, 1975.
Eva (Chava) Tenenbaum (Eva Romanowitz): numerous occasions including October 30, 1988; July 9, 1995; July 15, 1995; August 17, 1996; November 5, 1996; November 29, 1996; November 30, 1996.
Fryda Tenenbaum (Frieda Grayzel): July 8, 2012; July 11, 2012; July 18, 2012; August 16, 2012.
Jozef (Joe, Joseph) Tenebaum: numerous occasions including October 30, 1988; November 5, 1995; August 21, 1996; Octber 24, 1996; November 28, 1996; April 3, 1999.
Andzia Warzecha (Anna Tenenbaum): October 30, 1988.
Mania Warzecha (Miriam Romer): October 1, 1995.
Zlacia Warzecha (Sophie Samuels): numerous occasions including August 21, 1996; October 3, 1996; October 4, 1996; September 11, 2012.
Josef Zamulewicz (Joseph Samuels): numerous occasions including August 21, 1996; October 3, 1996; October 4, 1996; October 14, 1996; September 11, 2012.

Notes

Chapter 1

1. Wajsberg, *Sefer Zikaron Le-Kehilat Tomaszow Mazowiecki*, 291.
2. Mendes and de la Haye, *20th Century Fashion*, 92.
3. Wajsberg, *Sefer Zikaron Le-Kehilat Tomaszow Mazowiecki*, 322.
4. Pola, who lived in Radom, was a tall girl, very majestic in her appearance. During the war she was a courier for the Jewish underground resistance fighters.
5. Interview with Eva Romanowitz, July 15, 1995.
6. Wajsberg, *Sefer Zikaron Le-Kehilat Tomaszow Mazowiecki*, 247.
7. Yisrael Frankel, "The Yiddishe Professions and Their Organizations," in Wajsberg, *Sefer Zikaron Le-Kehilat Tomaszow Mazowiecki*, 216.
8. Gedalyihu Kesharowski, "Tomaszow's Hitradut Party and Gordonia," in Wajsberg, *Sefer Zikaron Le-Kehilat Tomaszow Mazowiecki*, 233.
9. Samuel D. Kassow, "Community and Identity in the Interwar Shtetl," in Gutman, *Jews of Poland*, 218.
10. A. Bugaiewicz, "Boleslaw Szeps," in Wajsberg, *Sefer Zikaron Le-Kehilat Tomaszow Mazowiecki*, 301.
11. Heller, *Edge of Destruction*, 44.
12. Jerzy Tomaszewski, "The Role of Jews in Polish Commerce, 1918–1939," in Gutman, *Jews of Poland*, 155.

Chapter 2

1. Lev Yanushevitz, "The Year 1939," Wajsberg, *Sefer Zikaron Le-Kehilat Tomaszow Mazowiecki*, 357.
2. Interview with Srulek (Israel) Rozanski, January 10, 1998.
3. Elimelech Garfinkel, "The Last Days of the Jewish Community," in Wajsberg, *Sefer Zikaron Le-Kehilat Tomaszow Mazowiecki*, 358.
4. Grobman, Landes, and Milton, *Genocide*, 12.
5. Kaiser, *Optimist Without Hope*, 53.

6. Only in late 1944 would Leibish finally be transported to Birkenau.
7. Interview with Josef Samulewicz, October 4, 1996.
8. Kaiser, *Optimist Without Hope*, 54–55.
9. Machel Grossman, "The *Aussiedlung* of 1942" ("Deportation of the Jews of Tomaszow-Mazowiecki"), translated by Morris Gradel, in Wajsberg, *Sefer Zikaron Le-Kehilat Tomaszow Mazowiecki*, 367.

Chapter 3

1. Ibid., 364.
2. Ibid.
3. "Treblinka."
4. Machel Grossman, "The Palestine Aktion" ("Operation Palestine"), in Wajsberg, *Sefer Zikaron Le-Kehilat Tomaszow Mazowiecki*, 373–74.
5. The yizkor book's editor intentionally did not publish the policeman's full name.
6. Grossman, "Purim Aktion," translated by Morris Gradel in Wajsberg, *Sefer Zikaron Le-Kehilat Tomaszow Mazowiecki*, 374–78.
7. Four months later, in September, they were sent to Starachowice, a labor camp near Radom.

Chapter 4

1. Kaiser, *Optimist Without Hope*, 85.
2. Nieuwsma, *Kinderlager*, 76.
3. Interview with Josef Zamulewicz who appeared in court on Heller's behalf. Interviewed September 11, 2012.

Chapter 5

1. Nazi camp records at Auschwitz-Birkenau Library.
2. Nieuwsma, *Kinderlager*, 80.
3. Nazi camp records at Auschwitz-Birkenau Library.
4. Nazi camp records at Auschwitz-Birkenau Library.
5. Kaiser, *Optimist Without Hope*, 131.
6. Testimony of Lazar Grejs, taken on June 3, 1986, in Auschwitz by Danuta Czech. Auschwitz-Birkenau Library.
7. Nieuwsma, *Kinderlager*, 85–86.
8. Interview with Joseph Tenenbaum, August 21, 1996.
9. Years later I would donate that suitcase to the Holocaust Center of Brooklyn.

Chapter 6

1. Death count from U.S. Holocaust Museum website: http://www.ushmm.org/wlc/en/article.php?ModuleId=10005224, accessed August 11, 2012.

Bibliography

Bacon, Gershon C. *The Politics of Tradition: Agudat Yisrael in Poland, 1916–1939*. Jerusalem: Magnes Press, Hebrew University, 1996.

"Bergen Belsen." United States Holocaust Memorial Museum. Holocaust Encyclopedia. http://www.ushmm.org/wlc/en/article.php?ModuleId=10005224. Accessed July 21, 2012.

Dawidowicz, Lucy S. *The War Against the Jews, 1933–1945*. New York: Holt, Rinehart and Winston, 1975.

Dean, Martin. *Collaboration in the Holocaust, Crimes of the Local Police in Belorussia and Ukraine, 1941–44*. New York: St. Martin's Press, 2000.

Gilbert, Martin. *The Holocaust: A History of the Jews of Europe during the Second World War*. New York: Holt, Rinehart and Winston, 1985.

Grobman, Alex, Daniel Landes, and Sybil Milton, eds. *Genocide: Critical Issues of the Holcaust*. Springfield, NJ: Behrman House, 1983.

Gutman, Yisrael, ed. *The Jews of Poland between the Two World Wars*. Hanover, NH: University Press of New England, 1989.

Heller, Celia. *On the Edge of Destruction*. Detroit, MI: Wayne State University Press, 1994.

Hillberg, Raul. *The Destruction of the European Jews*. New York: Holmes and Meier, 1985.

Kaiser, Wolf. *An Optimist Without Hope*. Brooklyn, NY: self-published, 1980.

Lower, Wendy. *Nazi Empire-Building*. Chapel Hill: University of North Carolina Press, 2005.

Mendelsohn, Ezra. *The Jews of East Central Europe*. Bloomington: Indiana University Press, 1983.

———. *Zionism in the Jewish Community of Poland During the 20's*. Spiegel Lectures in European Jewish History. Tel Aviv: Tel Aviv University, 1982.

Mendes, Valerie, and Amy de la Haye. *20th Century Fashion*. London: Thames and Hudson, 1999.

Moore, Deborah Dash, ed. *East European Jews in Two Worlds, Studies from the YIVO Annual*. Evanston, IL: Northwestern University Press, 1990.

Nieuwsma, Milton J., ed. *Kinderlager: An Oral History of Young Holocaust Survivors*. New York: Holiday House, 1998.

Shapiro, Robert Moses. *The Polish Kehile Elections of 1936: A Revolution Re-examined*. Working papers in Holocaust Studies. New York: Yeshiva University, September, 1988.

"Treblinka." U.S. Holocaust Memorial Museum. Holocaust Encyclopedia. http://www.ushmm.org/wlc/en/article.php?ModuleId=10005193. Accessed July 21, 2012.

Wajsberg, Moshe, ed. *Sefer Zikaron Le-Kehilat Tomaszow Mazowiecki*. [Tomaszow-Mazowiecki Yizkor Book.] Tel Aviv: Tomashow [sic] Organization in Israel, 1969.

Yaari-Wald, B., ed. *Irgun Jotzei Tomaszow-Mazoawiecki [sic] in Israel*. Tel Aviv: self-published, 1993.

Index

Page numbers in *italic* refer to illustrations.